Cooking California Style

Cooking California Style

BARBARA JOAN HANSEN

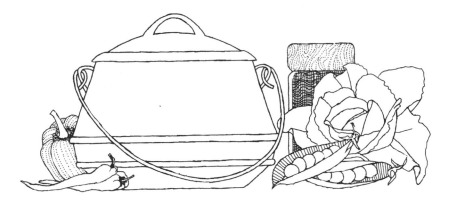

The Macmillan Company
New York, New York

The Macmillan Company
866 Third Avenue, New York, N.Y. 10022
Collier-Macmillan Canada Ltd., Toronto, Ontario

Library of Congress Catalog Card Number: 77–158167
First Printing
Printed in the United States of America

TO MOTHER

the best cook of all

Contents

INTRODUCTION

The typical Californian comes from anywhere in the world, and his cookery is equally diverse. Our culinary offerings extend far beyond the glorified hamburger and ever-burning barbecue which typify the California way of life to so many. The real California cuisine is eclectic, fascinating, and so varied that it is impossible to generalize about it. The best one can do is to say that we cook with the influence of Mexico and the Orient—our neighbors to the South and West—seasoned with a dash of any nationality you can think of and a generous pinch of Middle West common sense.

California is an exciting place to live and an exciting place to cook. Blue skies and balmy weather nourish a vigorous population and a natural bounty of good things to be turned into fresh and interesting dishes.

In this state we cook with a freedom that comes from lavish

supply unhampered by the constrictions of winter. In southern California, where I grew up, there is little sense of seasons, for in winter one may suddenly swelter through days of high temperatures and brilliant skies, while summer has long, cool, cloudy spells.

It is hard for me, therefore, to divide the year into distinct seasonal variations and to connect these with the presence or absence of certain foods in our markets. Sometimes the long green chiles are hotter than others. Occasionally I can't find a chayote, that delicate green squash fit for the most subtle of gourmets. In June markets begin to display the juicy little Thompson Seedless grapes, which reach their sweet pinnacle in August and September. And I know it is summer when green corn tamales, their dough made with corn grated right off the cob, appear on the menus at the Mexican restaurants.

The transition to fall is marked by sharp, clear skies and dry heat with a tinge of cold. This is the time for the apple harvests, and when the thirst for fresh cider grows strong, I drive to Oak Glen, a ruggedly picturesque community of orchards set against a mountain range some eighty miles from Los Angeles. Here one can picnic in the orchards, load up with jugs of cider unlike any that can be bought in markets, and stop for a slice of old-fashioned apple pie at such establishments as the Longbranch Pieloon.

To experience winter in its traditional, snowbound sense, many of us go skiing. These weekend excursions enhance our diets with an occasional hot buttered rum and much icy red wine from bottles which we bury in the snow and dig up again after an invigorating dash down the slopes.

But throughout the year, the pattern of eating in California remains basically the same—dinners accessorized with the prodigious green salads that are western classics and breakfasts that start with an orange, a grapefruit, some fresh papaya or pineapple, or figs from the tree.

If a particular item disappears from the markets for a time, enough else is available to send the inventive cook into a spin of confusion. All the cuisines of the world are represented on the shelves—an immense variety that has developed at the demand of our heterogeneous population. The people who developed this end of the continent came from throughout the United States and all over the world, bringing their recipes with them. There is no set pattern for California food, and there is no such thing as a typical California cook, unless it is someone who is open-minded and imaginative in the use of food.

Next door to me meals have a Romanian flavor; across the street, mixed South American; and down the block, French. One of my friends has a housekeeper from Chihuahua and dines in the manner of northern Mexico. Her neighbors are Japanese. Another friend of mine comes from Jogjakarta and spreads the culture of Indonesia with the aid of her pots and pans.

My own favorite cuisine is that of Mexico. But I am also fascinated by the high art of the French and refreshed by the light touch of the Chinese—all this with a Danish-Iowan heritage.

As basic in my kitchen as flour, butter and sugar are soy sauce, sesame oil, masa, dried chiles and fresh ginger root. Cooking to me is passion and fun, important enough to inspire the learning of extra languages so that I may study recipes that are not "adapted to American kitchens." In Los Angeles, where I live, few recipes require adapting, for almost any ingredient is available, from Jamaican ackees to Hawaiian poi.

We don't hunt for these things in specialty shops because they are not curiosities, but are everyday supplies required by large segments of the population. That earns them a place on super-market shelves. On one of my routes to downtown Los Angeles, I can pick up anything I need in Japanese supplies from several major chain markets. Coming back another way, I pass a Filipino neighborhood and then a "tortillería" where women pat out the meaty tortillas that are so much better for certain Mexican dishes than the thinner machine-made ones.

On the same block is a supermarket featuring Caribbean and Latin foods—fruit pastes, coconut syrup, fresh yuca, yautia and plantains, achiote, chiles, and cassava flour.

The mere presence of these exotics does not guarantee anything beyond average cookery, but the nature of the Californian does. The people who come here are root breakers, willing to try something new in the hope that it will be better, or at least, more interesting. Established ways have no power in themselves.

An irascible chef once shook a French cookbook at me, denounced a recipe that differed slightly from the traditional formula, and dismissed the author as an impostor. Such sacred conventions interest, but do not bind, the California cook. If a change of ingredients improved the dish, he would make the change. Experimentation is admired, but valid only if the result is good.

Californians are mobile people and their taste is not provincial. They travel up and down the state, over the border to Mexico, and around the world. And at home they recreate what they have seen and eaten.

Our most imaginative cooking is probably that done at home, for this is a land of self-expression. The creative atmosphere that draws artists, craftsmen, musicians, and writers here also permeates the kitchen. The restaurant chef, unfortunately, has problems of labor, economics, and mass appeal to consider when inspiration strikes.

From some points of view, Californians are a bit rough and ready—energetic perhaps, but not cultivated. A restaurateur once complained to me that Californians don't know how to dine. His reason? They don't wear dinner jackets when out on the town. Now, the day one's clothing determines the quality of one's food, I'll eat my pink cocktail dress and wear lobster bisque. Elegance and formality aren't necessarily related, and in California, the style of life is different. When we entertain at home and tell our guests to be informal, we generally mean slacks. But beautifully coordinated California sportswear is a long way from sloppy pants.

One of the most elegant evenings I can recall was spent at an isolated ranch in the Malibu mountains. The whitewashed house, built many years ago in the Mexican style, overlooked waves of golden hills that might have been untouched since the colorful days of the vaqueros. We sat outside under a vine arbor until twilight and then gathered around a huge fireplace of crackling logs for cocktails.

The household help consisted of a Mexican couple, neither of whom spoke English. The man, dressed for evening in formal black trousers and starchy shirt, summoned us to dinner, and we followed over tiled floors to a massive wooden table where, by candlelight, we ate quantities of smoke-barbecued beef and passed a "porron" filled with sparkling, deep red sangría. Our ranch clothes—sweaters, slacks and jeans—were as comfortable as the old hacienda, and we enjoyed without pretensions expansive hospitality reminiscent of another day.

Whenever I make sangría, the recipe for which you will find in chapter 7, I am back once again in that ranch house. The palate, as you have probably discovered, has as sensitive a memory for the joys of the past as the nose and ears. Through them an experience is not just remembered but relived as we taste, smell, or hear again some emotion-tinged aspect of the past.

Each time I prepare a dish with fresh ginger, I can smell the lovely, waxy, white ginger blossoms that I once bought in Hong Kong. And I can see that magnificent, sparkling harbor ringed by purply blue mountains that are not so different from the mountains that ring Los Angeles.

It was when I realized that cooking could be an art, a means of expressing a civilization and culture, that I gave in to the lures of the kitchen. There are few more dreary terms in our language than "domestic science" and "home economics." Feeding belongs under those headings, perhaps, but not the fascinating, individualistic art of cookery.

When I wrote down my first recipe, the setting was, appropriately, a turreted, high-ceilinged Pasadena mansion that had once housed California governors. And soon I was off, traveling through the world, up and down the east coast of Asia, to Mexico, the Caribbean and Central America, to many places in California and the Southwest, and vineyard touring in California, France, and Spain.

Travel gave me wonderful opportunities to taste, compare and talk about food, to write down new ideas, to study new ingredients and their uses. And it opened my eyes to interesting possibilities that I had overlooked at home. I never learned so much about my own city, it seemed, as when I began to investigate it from a culinary angle. But that is logical when you consider that food is the basis of human existence.

The recipes which follow are the results of those explorations. They are my response to a lively, multi-faceted environment, the expression of a personal style of cooking. You will find recipes that are wholly or in part Japanese, Indonesian, Chinese, Mexican, French, Spanish, Siamese, Hawaiian, Puerto Rican, Jamaican and, of course, American.

The intellect might regard blending so many styles of cooking as the sure way to indigestion. But then, intellects have a way of setting up barriers that prevent one from experiencing many pleasures. Trust instead to the palate and the eye. They will discover that dishes of diverse origins can mix and match quite logically. The idea that Chinese food goes only with other Chinese food is a fallacy. Don't judge a dish by its nationality, but by its basic essences. Is it sweet, spicy, heavy, light, colorful, or bland? Then relate those qualities to the rest of your menu.

Although some of the recipes in this book were collected abroad, they are none the less Californian, for in my journeys I only contacted the source of what I found at home.

When serving a meal of a distinctive nationality, I like to carry out the mood with placemats, accessories, and even, if possible, background music—a culinary eccentricity, perhaps. I remember once donning a cotton yukata and preparing sukiyaki to the accompaniment of Kabuki music, which makes about as much sense as a Japanese in Kyoto wearing blue jeans and frying hamburgers to Leonard Bernstein's *Candide*.

While preparing the following dishes, you may wear any attire, and you may serve them to any music, or none at all. I only hope that your horizons are widened and that you experience some sensation of what it is like to live in a sunny state where life and food are original and fun.

A NOTE TO THE COOK

AND A GLOSSARY

Many ingredients that are unfamiliar in some parts of the United States are called for in this book. They are not used to be exotic or different, but because they are basic parts of certain cuisines and worthy of more widespread recognition.

The use of these ingredients should not discourage the person who cannot readily obtain them. The primary factor in preparing any dish is the skill and versatility of the cook, and the resourceful cook is master of the recipe, not vice versa. If any ingredient is unavailable, the dish need not linger forever beyond reach. One merely eliminates the obscure item or substitutes, producing not an altered version of the recipe but an entirely new and perhaps superior dish.

For years I worried over Chinese recipes which called for an infinitesimal amount of chopped ham to enhance a main ingredient such as chicken. I finally learned not to skip the recipe or to wait for the day after serving baked ham, for when I had the ham, I usually couldn't remember by then what recipe had been so appealing. Wiser now, I try the recipe at once and forget the inconvenient tablespoon or two of chopped ham, and I have not yet suffered from the lack.

Certain of the less common ingredients used in this book can be duplicated easily. Nixtamal and canned hominy, for example, are basically the same thing, but using canned hominy eliminates the hours of simmering it takes to tenderize nixtamal.

You can also survive fairly well without five spice powder. Available in most Chinese markets, this spice has a strong anise flavor, and an adequate substitute would be a judicious pinch of aniseed.

Similarly, mirin is sweet sake (rice wine), and if you don't have mirin, you can use sake plus sugar. The substitute for sake would be a dry white wine or dry sherry.

There are two ingredients, however, that it is impossible to approximate. These are fresh ginger root and fresh coriander, an herb marketed in California under its Spanish name, cilantro. So heavenly and distinctive is the touch they add to a dish that I cannot conceive of cooking without them. Ground, preserved, or candied ginger taste quite different from the fresh, and coriander seeds cannot substitute for the green leaves they produce. In some gourmet departments, one can find expensive small cans of green ginger. And some green-thumbed cooks grow their own fresh coriander from the seeds. I plant it in September and again in early spring, harvesting my own seeds.

Those to whom these and the other special ingredients are new will find them explained in the glossary that follows.

ANGELICA.   A California dessert wine.

AONORIKO.   Powdered seaweed, a Japanese condiment.

ARARE.   Japanese rice crackers.

BUTTER LETTUCE.   A type of head lettuce that is softer, smoother in texture and less compact than iceberg lettuce.

CAPONATA.   An Italian relish of mixed vegetables including eggplant, tomatoes, onions, capers, and so forth.

CARNE SECA.   The Mexican version of jerked beef. Carne seca, which means dried meat, must be tenderized by pounding and can then be pulled apart and added to soups and other dishes.

CHAYOTE. A pear-shaped green squash that has as many names as it has uses. Its aliases include custard marrow, vegetable pear, christophene, cho cho, chu chu, and güisquil. Tender and delicately flavored, the chayote may be served as a vegetable or combined with meat for a main course. In Latin America, it is sometimes used as a dessert, and in the Caribbean, it is made into a mock applesauce. Chayotes come large and small, smooth skinned and with spines.

CHESTER CHEESE. A light-colored, Cheddar-type cheese used in Mexico for quesadillas and other dishes needing a flavorful cheese which won't run. The name stems from England's Cheshire cheese.

CHIA. Tiny seeds from a wild plant. Chia was gathered by Indians, is used by Mexicans for a refreshing drink, and is now popular with health food fanciers. Chia seed bread is available in health food stores.

CHICKEN SEASONED STOCK BASE. A powdered chicken broth base that is dissolved in hot water to make instant broth. It is stocked in the spice racks of most supermarkets.

CHILES. Fresh chiles (chile peppers) come either mild (California, also called long green chile, and poblano) or hot (serrano, jalapeño, güero). Canned chiles are a good substitute for the fresh, but the familiar green or bell pepper should not be substituted as it has a distinctive flavor of its own.

   The most common dried chiles are branded as California (mild) and New Mexico (hot). Others are ancho, mulato, pasilla, cascabel (hot) and pequin, also called tepin (violent).

   Chili powder may be substituted for dried chiles. It comes either hot or mild, pure and red, or dark and spiced. Crushed dried chiles are available on most spice racks, and an Indonesian condiment called sambal oelek, which is chiles ground to a paste, is handy to use if you can get it. Incidentally, chili is an American spelling applied generally to chili powder, chili meat and beans. Chile is the Spanish spelling.

CHINESE FIVE SPICE POWDER. A spice blend of star anise, anise pepper, cinnamon, cloves, and fennel. Anise is the dominant flavor. It is sold in Oriental markets.

CHINESE SAUSAGES. Rich pork sausages, which are long and slender. The Chinese often steam them over rice.

CHORIZO. Mexican chorizo is a highly spiced link sausage made with pork or beef or a combination of the two. Spanish chorizo is milder and different in flavor. In this book most of the recipes that call for chorizo mean the Mexican variety, not the Spanish.

CILANTRO. Fresh coriander. Sold in bunches in the same fashion as watercress and parsley, it is used liberally in Mexican cooking as an ingredient or a garnish. It is also used in Chinese cookery and is known to Orientalists as Chinese parsley. In Puerto Rico, you may see it spelled "culantro."

COCONUT MILK. The liquid obtained by steeping fresh or dried grated coconut in milk or water and wringing it through a cloth. It is not the same as coconut water, which is the liquid inside a coconut. In California, coconut milk is available in cans and is also flown in frozen from Hawaii.

DAIKON. A large, pungent white radish used extensively in Japanese cooking.

DASHI. A fish stock used in Japan as a clear soup or as a flavoring for other dishes.

GINGER ROOT. Fresh ginger comes in knobby roots with a thin brown skin. The skin is peeled off and the root is sliced, minced, or shredded for use in cookery.

GINGER SPROUTS. Long, thin red ginger sprouts in vinegar sold in jars in Japanese markets.

GOLDEN SYRUP. An English syrup similar to a light molasses.

GUAVA PASTE. Guava pulp cooked with sugar to a paste. It is formed into blocks and sold in Mexican and Caribbean markets.

JICAMA. A large root vegetable with a thin brown skin and pulp that is firm and faintly sweet. The jicama is popular in Mexico and is used by some Oriental cooks as a substitute for water chestnuts.

KETJAP. An Indonesian type soy sauce that is slightly sweet.

LEMON GRASS. An herb used in Southeast Asian cooking. A bushy perennial plant with long, slender leaves, it grows well in California. Powdered lemon grass is sold in markets with a Dutch-Indonesian trade. Dried lemon grass is available in some health food stores.

LEMON PEPPER MARINADE. This is not a liquid marinade, but a dry mixture of pepper, salt, lemon peel, and other seasonings. Look for it in supermarket spice racks or gourmet sections.

LONGANS. A small white fruit which is imported canned from Taiwan. Longans are similar in appearance to lychees, but are smaller and more delicate in flavor.

MARSALOVO. An Italian wine specialty based on Marsala wine and including a trace of egg. It is made in California.

MASA. The dough from which tortillas, tamales, and other Mexican corn snacks are made. Masa consists of dried corn that has been cooked with lime and then ground. A fine grind is used for tortillas and a coarser grind for tamales. Instant masa is a corn flour to which you add water to make the dough. The best-known brand is Masa Harina; a companion product is Masa Trigo, a mix for making flour tortillas.

MIRIN. Sweet sake.

NAPPA CABBAGE. Also called Chinese cabbage, nappa cabbage comes in a long bunch like celery and has white leaves with frilly, pale green tips.

NOPALES. Paddles of prickly pear cactus that are diced, cooked, and used in Mexican dishes. They are sold both fresh and canned in Mexican markets.

ORANGE SHELLS. Canned orange shells in syrup are served as a dessert in the Caribbean.

OYSTER SAUCE. A condiment used in Chinese cooking.

PATIS. Liquefied anchovy, a sauce that comes from the Philippines and is a handy condiment to add to salad dressings and sauces.

PILONCILLO. Hard cones of brown sugar sold in Mexican markets. Piloncillo is also called panocha and panela.

PLANTAINS. Called cooking bananas, plantains are used more as a vegetable than as a fruit. They are important in Latin and Caribbean cookery.

PON VINEGAR. A delicate, orange-flavored Japanese vinegar.

QUESO ASADERO. A mild white cheese that melts easily and is much used in Mexican cooking.

QUESO ENCHILADO. A crumbly, white Mexican cheese that looks like angel food cake, as it comes in blocks or wedges coated with red powder. It is crumbled over enchiladas and other dishes as a garnish.

RED LETTUCE.   A crinkly leaf lettuce that is deep red at the ends of the leaves.

SAKE.   Japanese rice wine.

SANSHO.   A Japanese pepper with a distinctive flavor.

SESAME BRITTLE.   Small, square candies made of sesame seeds, sugar, and honey.

SESAME OIL.   A pungent oil much used in Oriental cookery and found in most Oriental markets. Its nutty flavor is so strong that only a few drops are added to a dish. Do not substitute bland domestic sesame oils.

SHRIMP-FLAVORED CHIPS.   Imported from Hong Kong, the chips are little wafers that puff up into a delicious snack when deep fried.

SOY BEAN CURD.   Called tofu in Japanese markets, the curd is bland and firm like a stiff custard. It is sold canned or in blocks that are packed in water.

SOY SAUCE.   A salty condiment produced domestically and also imported from Hawaii, Hong Kong, and Japan. Brewed from the soy bean, soy sauce is essential to Oriental cooking and adds both saltiness and color.

STRING CHEESE.   A tubular form of mozzarella that can be pulled apart into strings. Popular with Armenians, it is generally marketed as Armenian string cheese.

TACO SEASONING MIX.   A common supermarket item which can be used not only to season taco filling, but also to flavor beans and other dishes.

TAHINI.   A soft, runny paste made from crushed sesame seeds and sold in Middle Eastern markets. Hommos tahini is a variation that includes ground garbanzo beans.

TELEME CHEESE.   A mild California cheese.

TILLAMOOK CHEESE.   An Oregon cheese that is similar to Cheddar.

TOMATILLOS.   Tiny green tomatoes with a parchment-like outer skin. Used in Mexican cooking, they are available both fresh and canned in California.

WATER CHESTNUTS.   A small, crisp Oriental vegetable most commonly available peeled and canned, but occasionally found fresh. The fresh water chestnuts are covered with a rough, brown skin, and when peeled, are sweeter and more crisp than those in cans.

1

Cocktails
and Appetizers

COCKTAILS

If the cocktail crowd made a pilgrimage, the destination would have to be California. After all, this is the state which gave birth to the martini, without which most cocktail parties, drinkers, joke makers, and gin salesmen would be out of business.

The martini is not Italian but, in a way, Mexican. Most drink historians agree that the drink was created by a San Francisco bartender a century ago. This man named his inspired mixture after the town of Martinez in nearby Contra Costa County. Martinez, in turn, was named after one Ignacio Martinez, who had been mayor of San Francisco in the 1830s.

It might seem surprising that the drink of sophisticates should have emerged from the wild and woolly West. But San Franciscans, although wild, were not exactly woolly. They quenched their thirst with some of the finest champagne California has ever produced—or so those with extra long memories say. And they drank Pisco sours long before travel agencies began to tout South America.

The martini has become the epitome of all cocktails. Wars, duels, and friendly combat take place over its every nuance. Should it be shaken or stirred; served on the rocks or off; garnished with an onion or an olive; and what should the olive be stuffed with?

The most crucial issue, of course, is the vermouth. How much should one add—a third, a fifth or a tenth part? Or should the bottle just be set within three, or perhaps five, feet of the pitcher while the drinks are being mixed?

Such jokes about the vermouth go on ad nauseam. The nauseam has inspired some drinkers to skip the vermouth, and extremists to forsake the martini entirely.

Ready to fill the gap was a bartender in Los Angeles. Some thirty years ago this resourceful man put together a drink that was a little bit salty, a little bit sweet, gentle in appearance, but with a forthright punch. His muse was a wealthy client named Margaret. So what else could the drink be called but Margarita—especially since it was based on that Mexican lightning called tequila?

Several rivals dispute our man's claim to have created the Margarita, and since the happening was so recent, historians are still weighing their arguments. But no matter who created it, the Margarita has risen to the levels of the martini, manhattan, old-fashioned, and gimlet as one of the most popular cocktails in the United States.

California produces lots of wine, but we leave the drinking of aperitifs to the French. And the French happily leave that custom at home when they come here. A French winemaker I know can't wait to get at the martinis when he comes to the United States on business. And a resident Frenchman still takes his Dubonnet, but with a gin base.

A more significant influence on California drinking is our proximity to another important liquid, the Pacific Ocean. Across this body of not very palatable water sailed the recipes for the rum drinks that are basic in Polynesian and Chinese restaurants up and down the coast.

When I attended Stanford University, the more daring daters

went to a jungle-enshrouded spot where they sipped a rum concoction so potent (to novices, that is) that only one or two drinks could be served per couple. This brew was presented in a bowl with two straws, and whoever was the stronger sipper got the most—and the worse hangover!

Nourished on such beverages, we Californians grow up with a taste for the exotic—mai tais, mango daiquiris, pearl divers, navy grogs, vicious virgins—and whatever else the menu writers can dream up.

These colorful and exotic drinks are sipped in tropical bowers (sometimes called bars) hung with lush foliage, with real or artificial squawking birds, waterfalls, and other South Pacific paraphernalia.

Tourists go wild over the fancy concoctions. But natives like them too, especially when long months of warm weather produce that balmy, relaxed, tropical feeling, and the palm trees, hibiscus, and bougainvillea make you feel that life—and drinks—should not always be strong and to the point.

California Martini

2 oz. gin (or more)
Dry vermouth to taste
Olive, onion, lemon twist, shrimp, cherry tomato, gherkin, chile pepper, tangerine segment, Japanese salty plum

Combine gin and vermouth. Stir with ice and serve in a stemmed or stemless cocktail glass, paper cup, or water tumbler. Decorate with 1 item from the list of garnishes. Makes 1 drink.

Saketini

With so many Japanese living in California, it was inevitable that this should happen to the martini. The ginger sprouts come in jars from Japan and are available in Japanese markets. Long, thin and red, they have to be trimmed down to fit the drink.

1½ oz. gin
¼ oz. sake
   Ginger sprouts in vinegar

Combine gin and sake and stir with ice. Strain and serve in a
cocktail glass with a ginger sprout as garnish. Makes 1 drink.

Strawberry Martini

Here is that rare combination, a pretty drink which is straight-
forward enough to please a man's taste.

1 part French strawberry vermouth
3 parts vodka
1 fresh strawberry for each drink

Combine vermouth and vodka and stir with ice until chilled. Pour
into a stemmed cocktail glass and garnish with the fresh strawberry.
Makes 1 drink.

Margarita

It would seem more Mexican to make this drink with fresh lime
juice, but the sweetened, bottled lime juice actually gives a better
flavor.

1 lime
   Salt
3 oz. tequila
1 oz. Rose's lime juice
1 oz. Cointreau
2–4 ice cubes, crushed

Rub the rims of 2 stemmed cocktail glasses with a freshly cut
lime and swirl the edge of each glass in a pile of salt. Place tequila,
lime juice, Cointreau and ice in a blender and blend until foamy.
Pour into the crusted cocktail glasses and serve. Makes 2 drinks.

Flor de la Selva

Not all of our tequila goes into Margaritas. This pale pink drink is as pretty as its name, which means jungle flower.

3 oz. tequila
1½ oz. pineapple-grapefruit juice
1 oz. fresh lime juice
½ oz. black currant syrup or crème de cassis

Combine ingredients in a cocktail shaker and shake with ice until chilled. Strain and serve over ice cubes. Makes 2 drinks.

Orange County Cocktail

The population explosion is crowding the orange trees out of Orange County, which borders Los Angeles County. But enough trees still flourish to provide inspiration for this drink.

1½ oz. bourbon
½ oz. mirin (sweet sake)
3 drops orange bitters
Orange peel

Pour the bourbon, mirin and bitters over ice in a cocktail glass and twist in the orange peel. Makes 1 drink.

We grow apples in California and make potent use of the crop, as the following two drinks indicate. At Oak Glen, which is in southern California, they make cider so good you can hardly stop drinking it—a dangerous situation after vodka has been added. Sebastopol, in northern California, produces apple brandy as well as cider and juice. Combine them and you'll keep the doctor away—unless you offer him a drink too.

Oak Glen Apple Knocker

A waste of good cider and liquor.

1½ oz. vodka
1½ oz. fresh apple cider

Combine and serve over ice. Makes 1 drink.

Sebastopol Brandy Cocktail

1½ oz. apple brandy
¾ oz. apple juice
1 drop Angostura bitters

Combine and serve on the rocks. Makes 1 drink.

Gin and Two

This drink is English, but there is nothing conservative about it.

1½ oz. gin
1 oz. dry vermouth
½ oz. sweet vermouth

Combine gin and the two vermouths and stir with ice until chilled. Makes 1 drink.

My Brandy Manhattan

When I toured the Far East on a freighter, I took on board one bottle each of California brandy, California vermouth, and Angostura bitters. The brandy ran out between Bangkok and Hong Kong, the vermouth made the whole trip, and I still have the bitters. This is the drink I mixed.

1½ oz. brandy
½ tsp. dry vermouth
1 drop Angostura bitters
1 ice cube

Combine brandy, vermouth and bitters in a cocktail glass and add the ice cube. Makes 1 drink.

Hong Kong Old-Fashioned

Old-fashioneds are often watery and insipid, but this one isn't. It is based on the prettiest old-fashioned I have ever seen, which was served at the Miramar Hotel in Kowloon.

Few drops of bar syrup
2 drops Angostura bitters
1½ oz. bourbon
2 ice cubes, coarsely crushed
1 slice of orange
1 maraschino cherry

In a cocktail glass, combine the bar syrup and bitters. Add the bourbon and ice. Cut the orange slice in quarters and float them in the drink. Garnish with a cherry. Makes 1 drink.

Note: To make bar syrup, combine 1 cup sugar, 1 cup water and 1 tablespoon light corn syrup. Bring to a boil and boil about 5 minutes. Cool and bottle.

Boggan's Irish Gimlet

I have an Irish friend who stages lavish St. Patrick's Day celebrations in Santa Monica. Everything is green, including the foam on the Irish coffee. The festivities start with this emerald drink.

Green food color
Green cherries
3 parts vodka or gin
1 part Rose's lime juice

Take enough water to fill a sectioned ice tray and tint it green with a few drops of food color. Pour the water into the tray, place a cherry in each section, and freeze. Combine the vodka and lime juice in a pitcher or jar, also with a little green food color. Serve each drink with 1 or 2 green ice cubes.

Kir

A California kir should be made with freshly squeezed pomegranate juice, which is so rich, thick, and fragrant, it is like a liqueur. Since the pomegranate season is short, we make it the rest of the year in the French fashion, with crème de cassis or black currant syrup.

3 oz. chilled California Chablis
1½–2 tsp. black currant syrup of crème de cassis

Combine wine and syrup and serve in a wine glass, with or without ice. Makes 1 drink.

Fresh Pineapple Daiquiri

When the weather turns warm, we turn to drinks like this. The pineapple dissolves completely in the blender, producing a glamorous, golden, foamy cocktail that makes one dream of a tropical island.

1 thick slice of fresh pineapple
3 oz. light rum
Juice of ½ lime
2 tsp. sugar
4 ice cubes, crushed

Place pineapple in the blender and add the rum, lime juice, sugar, and ice. Blend until foamy. Serve over ice with straws. Makes 2 tall drinks or 3 short ones.

Fresh Strawberry Daiquiri

This is luscious and looks spectacular when served in a hollow-stemmed champagne glass.

    ¼ cup mashed strawberries
        Sugar
    3 oz. rum
    1 oz. Cointreau
        Juice of ½ lime
    4 ice cubes, crushed
        Mint sprigs

When mashing the strawberries, add a little sugar. Place berries in blender and add rum, Cointreau, lime juice and ice. Spin until foamy. Serve in hollow-stemmed champagne glasses with a mint sprig as garnish. To remove the strawberry seeds, pour the drink through a fine sieve. Makes 2 drinks.

Golden Daiquiri

Dark rum adds a pungency that makes the daiquiri better than ever.

    1½ oz. light rum
    1½ oz. dark rum
         Juice of ½ lime
    ½ tsp. bar syrup, or to taste

Shake with ice and add 1–2 ice cubes to each serving. Makes 2 drinks.

Waikiki Rum Cooler

If you serve this to guests, you'll be imprisoned in the kitchen mixing more.

    1 oz. pineapple-grapefruit juice
    1 oz. guava nectar
    ½ oz. lemon juice
      Squeeze of lime juice
    1 oz. light rum
    1 oz. dark rum
    ½ tsp. orange curaçao
    ¾ tsp. grenadine syrup
    3 ice cubes, crushed
    ½ slice of orange, a cherry and fresh mint

Combine fruit juices, rums, curaçao, grenadine, and ice in a tall glass. Garnish with the half slice of orange and the cherry combined on a cocktail pick and a sprig of fresh mint. Makes 1 drink.

Papaya Dawn

Pale and cool as dawn, this is a drink for tropical summer days.

    2 oz. light rum
    1½ oz. dark rum
    1 oz. Cointreau
    ½ papaya, peeled, seeded, and sliced
    5 chunks of fresh pineapple
      Juice of ½ lime
    4–5 ice cubes, crushed

Combine rums, Cointreau, fruit, lime juice, and ice in the blender and whirl until frothy. Makes 3 drinks.

Panama Pink Gin

If you're ever steamed your way through the Panama Canal, you know how welcome a drink like this would be in that torrid region.

3 oz. gin
2 oz. pineapple juice
   Juice of ½ lime
   Few drops of grenadine syrup

Shake with ice until chilled and serve over 1–2 ice cubes. Makes 2 drinks.

Marsala Milk Punch

Along the Sunset Strip in Los Angeles, there are little cafés where you can while away an evening over espresso coffee, a cappuccino, or a wine-laced milk shake like this.

1 cup milk
1½ oz. Marsalovo or Marsala wine
1 tsp. sugar
¾ cup cracked ice

Combine milk, wine, sugar, and ice in a blender and whir until foamy. Add more sugar, if desired. Serve in tall glasses. Makes 2 drinks.

Stan's Germ Destroyer

When a cold gets you down, get up again with this.

1 cup hot tea
2 oz. bourbon
1 tbsp. honey

Pour the tea into a large mug, add the bourbon and stir in the honey until it melts. The tea should be as hot as possible. After drinking this, go to bed immediately. Makes 1 drink.

El Rey Alfonso

Dinner in Baja California often ends with a Kahlúa cocktail instead of a dessert. This Ensenada version of a King Alphonse is served on the rocks.

¾ oz. Kahlúa
¾ oz. brandy
2 tsp. heavy cream

Combine Kahlúa and brandy in a cocktail glass. Add 1 ice cube and float the cream on top. Makes 1 drink.

APPETIZERS

Never drink alone, and by that I mean have something to nibble on with your cocktails. The sharp, clean taste of alcohol can be too cutting when you're empty. It needs the contrast of food. However, I'm not one for swamping my guests with irresistible tidbits before dinner. A meal owes much of its allure to hunger, and I want good appetites at my table. My style is to serve one type of appetizer, or two at the most, and to keep them very simple. The cocktail hour is not the time to show off your cooking ability unless you are hosting one of those endless events that substitute for dinner rather than precede it. I've been to parties where I gasped at the bountiful selection of caviar, canapés, pâtés, and other goodies. But after a few mouthfuls, the rich combination would pall, and I would long only for a cup of tea to sooth the confusion in my stomach. I also feel that when you've spent hours on a menu, fussing over complicated little canapés can be the chore that destroys the enjoyment of the project. Therefore, this section emphasizes appetizers that take almost no work and yet will distinguish you from the unimaginative hostess who merely "pours out a bag of chips."

Shrimp Chips

In Chinese markets, you can find boxes labeled shrimp-flavored chips, containing thin, hard wafers about the size of a quarter or fifty-cent piece. You drop the wafers in hot oil, and they puff up many times their size and become light and crunchy—rather like a potato chip, but not greasy.

I consider shrimp chips the perfect appetizer, as they are mild in flavor and go with every type of drink. You can buy them ready puffed, but they taste better and fresher if you do it yourself. They are also convenient because you can fry a large batch and store them in airtight containers, where they will keep for days. Made from tapioca starch, shrimp meat and salt, the chips are inexpensive and come in assorted colors for a decorative effect.

Garlic Carrot Sticks

These are for garlic fans only. Scrape a carrot and cut it crosswise in 2 or 3 sections, depending on its length. Then cut each section into sticks. Place the sticks in a pint jar, fill the jar with water, and add a garlic clove that you have crushed to a paste with salt. Cover the jar and place it in the refrigerator for several hours. Then drain the sticks and serve them with a dip or by themselves. I like to stand the sticks in a little silver mug with a sprig of parsley at one side.

Chinese Sausages

The Chinese sausages I buy are made in Canada! Wipe the sausages with a damp cloth and steam them for about 45 minutes, or until thoroughly cooked. Cut the cooked sausages into 1½-inch slices and spear each on a toothpick. These are a bit greasy, so provide crackers or other dry snacks as a contrast.

Arare

Arare are small, crisp rice crackers sold in Japanese markets. They are salty with a hint of sweetness and a touch of seaweed for unusual flavor. Serve them instead of pretzels. They are great with beer.

Shortcut Rumaki

Chicken livers are customary with rumaki, a Polynesian appetizer of bacon wrapped around a chunk of liver and a water chestnut. However, I don't like them and so developed this version.

Soy sauce
Mirin
Garlic powder
Sugar
Water chestnuts
Bacon strips

Make a marinade by combining equal parts of soy sauce and mirin. Add a dash of garlic powder and enough sugar to make the mixture faintly sweet. Marinate water chestnuts in this mixture for an hour. Wrap each in a strip of bacon and secure with a toothpick. Return to the marinade for ½ hour, then drain, sprinkle with sugar and broil until the bacon is crisp.

Pineapple and Prosciutto

I encountered this appetizer on a flight from Los Angeles to Honolulu. Take bite-size chunks of fresh pineapple, wrap each in a thin strip of prosciutto and secure with a toothpick—refreshing, tasty and easy.

Pineapple-Bacon Pupus

Pupu is a term for appetizer which has drifted to California from Hawaii.

Canned pineapple slices
Bacon strips
Brown sugar
Dark rum

Cut the pineapple slices into chunks. Wrap each chunk in a bacon strip and secure with a toothpick. Place the appetizers in a baking pan and sprinkle them generously with brown sugar and a few drops of dark rum. Broil until browned on one side, then turn and brown the other side. When the bacon is crisp, tilt the pan and let the grease drain to one side. The trick is to scrape up the syrupy residue before it has hardened and place a little on each appetizer.

Prunes and Bacon

I first tasted this popular appetizer at a garden party given by the consul general of the Philippines in Los Angeles.

12 prunes
2 tbsp. sugar
6 slices of bacon

Cover the prunes with water and simmer gently for 1 hour. Add the sugar and simmer 1 hour longer. Drain the prunes, cut in halves and remove the pits. Cut each bacon slice crosswise in halves and lengthwise in halves, forming four pieces. Wrap each prune half in a bacon piece, fastening with a toothpick. Place under the broiler or bake at 350° until the bacon is cooked. Drain on a paper towel. Makes 2 dozen.

String Cheese

Armenians introduced me to the tubular form of mozzarella called "string cheese." It shreds naturally, so you pull it apart in fine strings and heap the strings on a plate. That is the way it is served at Armenian weddings and other parties.

Plantain Chips

These are the "potato chips" of Central America and the Caribbean. Peel a plantain and slice paper-thin with a vegetable slicer. Soak the slices in ice water. Heat oil in a small saucepan and drop in the drained slices, a few at a time. Fry until crispy and golden. Drain on paper towels and sprinkle with salt.

Tostada Chips

Using scissors, cut corn tortillas into 1-inch pieces. Fry these in hot lard or oil until browned. Drain the tostada chips and toss them in a paper bag with salt, garlic powder and chili powder.

Bocaditos

Bocadito is Spanish for little mouthful, and these are tiny tortillas topped with cheese and chili powder or chile strips. They are made with instant masa, the flour used by Mexican cooks to speed the making of tortillas.

¼ tsp. salt
½ cup instant masa
3½ tbsp. water, about
  Grated Cheddar cheese
  Chili powder
  Strips of canned hot green chile

Add salt to the masa and mix in enough water to make a spongy, moist dough. (The dough dries quickly as you work it and may need more water.) Divide the dough in thirds. One at a time, form each third into a ball, press into a patty and then pat out as thin as possible. Use the heel of the hand and pat the dough out on waxed paper so you can remove it easily. Cut the dough into circles with a small cooky or biscuit cutter. Bake the circles on a hot, ungreased griddle. After baking, wrap them in waxed paper and then in plastic wrap to keep them from drying out. When ready to use, top the circles with cheese and sprinkle with chili powder. Or top them with a chile strip and cover with cheese. Bake at 350° for 5–10 minutes, or until the cheese is melted and bubbly. Makes 2 dozen 1¼-inch canapés.

Hot Cheese Balls with Brandy

Use the pure red chili powder for these rather than the dark spiced type.

1 cup grated sharp Cheddar cheese
1½ oz. cream cheese
½ tsp. hot pepper sauce
1 tsp. brandy
  Chili powder

Work the Cheddar cheese and cream cheese together with a fork and blend in the hot pepper sauce and brandy. Form the mixture into balls the size of a marble and dust with chili powder. Accompany with small, plain crackers and provide toothpicks for spearing. Makes about 30.

Salad on the Rocks

You may think vegetable relishes are unimaginative, but dieters appreciate them. For a dramatic presentation, heap a huge bowl with crushed ice and arrange a forest of carrot sticks, celery sticks, cauliflowerets, green onions, radishes and green pepper strips over the top. Place a bowl of thousand island dressing or any tangy dip in the center for the non-dieters.

2

Soups

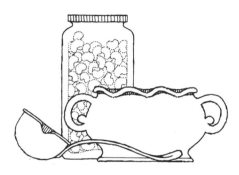

The alchemy of cookery manifests itself best in soups, those magical potions that cooks who rely on the can or the soup mix neither understand nor experience.

The climate where I live is warm, and for that reason I grew up without much interest in soups. My only encounters were with the canned or dried products, and while these brews were palatable and sometimes quite good, they gave no inkling of the wonders and subtleties that can be expressed in liquid form.

Then one day I came across a Mexican recipe for a tomato broth with apples. Such an unlikely combination had to be tested, and I set to work simmering and seasoning. The result, which I sampled immediately, was a light tomato broth with chunks of apple— good but not extraordinary.

I bottled what was left, put it in the refrigerator, and forgot about it. Five days later I was sure the soup had spoiled and should be thrown out. But thriftiness triumphed, and I tried another bowl. And what a surprise! This time I tasted not a tomato broth with apples but a magical amalgamation of flavors, a perfect blending of the ingredients into an entirely different and delicious creation.

Such was my introduction to soup making, and from then on I was fascinated by what had once seemed a humdrum aspect of cookery.

More experiments brought another surprise—how simple it can be to make a good soup. Infinite variations are possible, and one can work freely, tossing in an ingredient here and there without worrying about exact amounts.

What is important is a good, homemade stock (although, like most practical cooks, I am never without canned broth and prepared stock bases). The quality of the stock is particularly important in a soup like Consommé al Jerez, where it plays almost a solo role. Fortunately, stock making is even simpler than soup making, and the freezer makes it possible to keep a supply on hand.

I like to serve soup in small portions as a first course. A fine soup at the start of a meal excites the palate and makes the guests happy they came. If the soup is exceptionally good, it will condition your guests to enjoy a later dish. On the other hand, start with a poor soup, and the rest of the meal will have to work that much harder.

Keep the portions small, for the aim is to arouse the appetite, not dull it. The serving dishes are also important. I don't care for the shallow plates favored by some epicures. Soups should be either scaldingly hot or icily cold, and the broad, shallow plate dissipates the temperature. I either warm my bowls with hot water or chill them in the freezer, depending upon the nature of the soup.

My favorite containers are small black bowls from Japan, artfully shaped, with a pale gray interior and gray white lids. The soups are ladled in the kitchen and brought quickly to the table, their aroma and richness withheld for a tantalizing moment until the lid is lifted.

Here are some of the soups most likely to be unveiled in those bowls. Exotic, familiar, Japanese, Mexican, French, Chinese, American or mongrel, they reflect accurately their kaleidoscopic environment and illustrate in small measure the wide range of soup-making possibilities.

Two Basic Soup Stocks

Soup stock recipes with discouragingly long lists of ingredients generally wind up unused. Here are two simple formulas that rely on the ingredients most likely to be at hand. Embellish them as you please. Both can be frozen and kept indefinitely.

Simple Chicken Stock

3–4 lbs. chicken backs and necks
6 cups water
1 onion
1 tsp. salt

Buy the backs and necks from your butcher or use chicken bones you have on hand. Cover the bones with the water; add the onion, cut in chunks, and the salt. Simmer for 2 hours. Strain the stock and let cool. Fat will rise to the top after the stock is cold and can easily be removed. Makes about 1 quart stock.

Basic Beef Stock

6 lbs. beef bones and trimmings
3 quarts water
2 carrots
1 small onion
1 stalk celery
1 tbsp. salt

Cover the bones and trimmings with the water. Add the vegetables, cut in chunks, and the salt. Simmer for 4–5 hours. Strain into jars and cool. Skim off the fat after it hardens. Makes about 2½ quarts stock.

Cazuela

Cazuela and caldillo are two authentically Mexican soups that require the leathery dried beef called "carne seca." This meat comes in strips and must be pounded on the "metate" or in the "molcajete" (Mexican grinding devices made of stone) until it can be shredded. It is then simmered with the rest of the ingredients.

Cazuela, which means casserole, is a typical soup from the state of Sonora. Mrs. Maria Rojas brought the recipe for caldillo to Los Angeles from her ranch home in Chihuahua.

A good substitute for the carne seca in both recipes would be cooked, shredded chuck.

¾–1 cup shredded carne seca or shredded stewed beef chunks
1 tbsp. lard
1 onion
1 clove garlic
¼ tsp. salt
1 long green chile, peeled and seeded
1 medium tomato
1 quart beef stock
¼ cup coarsely chopped cilantro
Freshly ground black pepper

Pound the carne seca until tender and shred it as fine as possible. Melt the lard in a skillet and fry the onion, chopped fine, and the garlic, minced and mashed in the salt. Chop the chile and add when the onion is wilted. If the chile is hot, reduce the amount considerably. Now add the tomato, peeled and chopped, and the shredded meat. Simmer gently for 10 minutes.

Bring the beef stock to a boil. Add the fried mixture, the cilantro and a sprinkling of pepper. Simmer, covered, for about 3 hours. Test for seasoning and add more salt if necessary. Makes 6 first course servings.

Caldillo

¾–1 cup shredded carne seca or shredded stewed beef chunks
  1 small onion
  1 medium tomato
  1 clove garlic
  ¼ tsp. salt
  1 tbsp. butter
  ⅛ tsp. cumin
    Freshly ground black pepper
  1 quart beef stock
  1 small boiling potato
  1 tsp. cornstarch
  2 tsp. water

Pound the carne seca until tender and shred it as fine as possible. Chop the onion; peel and chop the tomato. Mince the garlic and mash with the salt. Melt the butter and sauté the onion and garlic until the onion is wilted. Add the tomato and meat. Sprinkle with the cumin and a little pepper and simmer together for 5 minutes.

Bring the beef stock to a boil and add the meat and vegetables. Simmer for about 3 hours. Peel and cube the potato, and add during the last hour of cooking. Simmer until the potato is tender. Test for seasoning. Add the cornstarch dissolved in the water and boil a few minutes longer. Serves 6.

Guacamole Soup

Too many avocado soups are bland and unexciting, but nothing with a Mexican touch is ever dull, as this excitingly flavored, liquid guacamole will prove.

½ avocado
2 tsp. lemon juice
1 cup half-and-half
1–2 tbsp. coarsely chopped green chile
1 small clove garlic
3 tbsp. chopped onion
2 tbsp. cilantro
1 cup light chicken stock
½ tsp. salt

This soup is made entirely in the blender. Start by blending the avocado with the lemon juice. Next add the half-and-half and blend again. Now add the chile (reduce the amount if it should be hot), the garlic, onion, and cilantro and blend again. Lastly, add the chicken stock and blend. Test for seasoning before adding the salt. If the chicken stock is salty, you may not need so much.

Serve the soup very cold with additional cilantro leaves as garnish. Makes 4 first-course servings.

NOTE: It is best to serve this soup on the day it is made and not to hold it over.

Chicken-Chile Soup, Mérida Style

One often finds good things in unlikely places. Taking a chance on a food stall at a park in Mérida, the capital of Yucatán, I came upon this ambrosial chicken soup. Mexico, of course, is famous for its soups, and this one is filled with bits of good things in exciting contrast—chicken meat, strips of hot chile, and instead of croutons, crisp brown chips of fried tortillas.

1 small onion
1 long green chile
1 tbsp. butter
1 quart chicken broth
1 cup shredded cooked chicken
  Salt and pepper
4 corn tortillas
2 tbsp. lard

Slice the onion in paper thin rounds. Cut each round in quarters. Peel, seed, and slice the chile in strips about ¼-inch wide and 1-inch long. Test the chile for strength. If mild, use the whole chile; if hot, reduce the portion considerably.

Sauté the onion and chile in the butter until cooked but not browned. Add to the chicken broth along with the shredded meat. Season with salt and pepper to taste and simmer.

Meanwhile, cut the tortillas, using kitchen scissors, into strips about ¼-inch wide and 1-inch long. Melt the lard in a skillet and fry the tortilla strips until brown and crisp. Drain on a paper towel.

When ready to serve, bring the soup to a boil. Scatter a handful of tortilla strips in each pre-warmed bowl. Pour the soup over and serve. Makes 6 servings.

Consommé al Jerez

If you order this consommé in Jerez, Spain, where the sherries are made, the waiter will bring the soup and then reach for a bottle of sherry from the bar and tip it generously into the bowl.

Since the presentation is half the fun, I suggest it as part of the recipe. Either pour the sherry direct from the bottle or try it my way—serve a liqueur glass containing the sherry with each bowl of soup and let the guest pour it in for himself.

¼ cup top-quality consommé or beef broth per serving
1 tbsp. dry sherry per serving

Bring the consommé to a boil and serve in small bowls accompanied by a liqueur glass of sherry to be poured into the soup. The consommé will benefit greatly from enrichment by any good leftover clear meat gravy.

Black Bean and Chorizo Soup

Many Cubans have settled in Los Angeles, bringing with them such favorite foods as black bean soup, "Moors and Christians" (black beans and rice), and Dulce de Coco (coconut dessert—see Chapter 6). In response to its new environment, this black bean soup has acquired a Mexican accent, or at least a spicy Mexican chorizo. Rich and aromatic, it is about the best bean soup I've tasted and needs only a good green salad and chunks of French bread as companions at the dinner table.

1 cup black beans
¼ tsp. baking soda
1 ham hock
1 medium onion
1 bay leaf
2 cloves garlic
¾ tsp. salt
½ tsp. oregano
⅛ tsp. cumin seeds
1 chorizo

Cover the beans with 2 quarts hot water and soak overnight. In the morning, drain the beans, rinse, and cover again with hot water. Bring to a full boil, adding the baking soda just before the boiling point is reached. Drain and cover once more with 2 quarts hot water. Add the ham hock, the onion, cut in chunks, and the bay leaf. Mash the garlic cloves in the salt and add along with the oregano and cumin.

Simmer the beans until tender. When the beans are nearly done (they should simmer most of the day), remove casing from chorizo and fry until brown and crumbly. Drain off the grease and add the chorizo to the soup. When the beans are tender, take out the ham hock and bay leaf and put the beans and other ingredients through a food mill. Cut the meat off the ham hock and add to the soup after it has been puréed, if you like. Cool the soup and bottle. Recipe makes about 5 cups soup.

NOTE: This soup should stand at least a day in order to develop its full flavor.

Hot Pea Potage

Chile seeds are hot, and most recipes instruct one to remove the seeds before using the chiles. This recipe, on the contrary, calls for a judicious amount of seeds—enough to add a barely perceptible touch of heat and that indefinable something that makes a simple soup something beyond the ordinary.

      2 ham hocks
   2½ quarts water
      2 carrots
      ½ onion
      1 heaping cup split peas
      1 clove garlic
      1 bay leaf
      4 peppercorns
      4 cloves
    18 seeds from a dried hot chile pepper (they will measure less
         than ⅛ tsp.)
      1 cup canned tomatoes
         Salt

Place the ham hocks and water in a deep soup pot. Add the carrots and onion, cut in chunks. Wash the split peas and add. Now put in the garlic, bay leaf, peppercorns, cloves, and chile seeds. Bring to a boil and simmer for about 5 hours. Then add the canned tomatoes. Simmer for another ½ hour. Remove the ham hocks and put the soup through a food mill or sieve, taking out the bay leaf and cloves. Cut the meat from the ham hocks and add to the puréed soup. Test for seasoning and add salt to taste. Makes 2 quarts soup.

Carrot-Brandy Soup

The carrot deserves better treatment than it usually gets, and this brandy-mellowed soup shows how it will react under the right circumstances.

3 medium carrots
1 onion
1 clove garlic
¼ tsp. salt
1 tbsp. butter
1 tbsp. brown sugar
1½ tbsp. tomato purée
1 quart chicken stock
Pinch of rosemary
Salt and pepper to taste
1 tbsp. brandy

Scrape the carrots, cut them into rounds or strips and boil in salted water for 15 minutes; drain. Chop the onion and mash the garlic in the salt. Sauté the onion and garlic in the butter until the onion is wilted. Add the drained carrots, sprinkle with the brown sugar, and stir in the tomato purée.

Add the vegetables to the chicken stock along with the rosemary and simmer for ½ hour. Purée through a food mill or sieve. Check for seasoning and add salt and pepper to taste. Continue to simmer for at least 1 hour. Just before serving, add the brandy. Makes 6 servings.

The French have added substantially to good taste in California, both as vineyardists and restaurateurs. The following three cream soups are typically French, but the first two have a California touch in the subtle flavor of cilantro as the garnish.

My first taste of Potage Parmentier came, not in Paris but in Los Angeles, at what could only be called a California-style French restaurant. Called The Tower, it stands thirty-two stories high, glass enclosed, gazing west to the Pacific Ocean and Hollywood Hills, and elegantly aloof from the mad maze of freeways below.

Potage Parmentier

    2 leeks, white part only
 1½ lbs. boiling potatoes
    2 tbsp. butter
    6 cups water
    2 tsp. salt
    ½ cup milk
    2 tsp. chicken-seasoned stock base
    2 eggs yolks
    ½ cup cream
       Butter
       Cilantro
       Croutons

Wash the leeks thoroughly to remove all sand. Cut the white part in thin slices. Peel the potatoes, cut in thick slices, and immerse in cold water until needed.

Sauté the leeks in the butter until soft but not browned. Bring the water to a boil with 1 teaspoon of the salt. Add the leeks and the drained potato slices. Keep at a low boil for 1 hour, or until the potatoes are cooked. Put the soup through a food mill or mash through a sieve.

Return the soup to the stove and add the milk, the chicken-seasoned stock base, and the remaining salt. Simmer for another hour. Test for seasoning and add more salt if necessary.

Beat the egg yolks in a small bowl. Add the cream, and slowly pour a little of the soup into the egg mixture. Add the egg yolks to the soup pot and bring to a boil.

Warm the soup bowls. Place 1 teaspoon butter in each. Pour the boiling soup over and sprinkle with coarsely chopped cilantro or parsley. Croutons may also be added. Serves 8–10.

Crème Dubarry

1 leek, white part only
1 small clove garlic
¼ tsp. salt
3 tbsp. butter
½ small cauliflower
2 tbsp. flour
3 cups water
½ cup half-and-half
  Salt to taste
1 egg yolk
¼ cup cream
  Croutons
  Chopped cilantro or parsley

Slice the leek; crush the garlic in salt; and sauté both in 1 table-spoon butter until the leek is wilted. Break the cauliflower into flowerets and parboil in salted water 8 minutes. Drain and rinse with cold water.

Melt 2 tablespoons butter in a soup pot. Blend in the flour. Slowly add 1 cup water, stirring constantly until the flour-butter mixture dissolves. Add the rest of the water and bring to a boil. Add the leek, garlic, and cauliflowerets. Simmer 45 minutes. Purée through a food mill or sieve.

Return the soup to the stove and add the half-and-half. Season to taste with salt and simmer for ½ hour. Just before serving, beat the egg yolk, add the cream, and pour into the soup mixture, adding a little soup to the egg first to prevent curdling. Garnish with croutons and cilantro or parsley. Makes 6 first course servings.

Potage au Cresson
(*Watercress Soup*)

2 large green onions
1 bunch watercress
2 tbsp. butter

3 cups chicken stock
1 boiling potato
1 clove garlic
1 cup milk
   Salt to taste
1 egg yolk
¼ cup cream

Chop the onions and sauté with the watercress in the butter until wilted. Bring the stock to a boil. Add the onions, watercress, the potato, peeled and sliced, and the garlic clove. Simmer for an hour, or until the potato is thoroughly cooked. Remove the garlic clove and put the vegetables through a food mill or sieve. Add the milk to the soup and test for seasoning, adding salt as needed. Simmer for ½ hour. Beat the egg yolk, combine with the cream, and pour into the soup mixture, adding a little soup to the egg first to prevent curdling. Makes 1 quart.

Caldo Verde
(*Green Soup*)

The secret of this Portuguese soup is to add the kale just before serving and not to let it cook more than a minute in the soup. Then you will have the beautiful fresh green color that gives the soup its name.

1 lb. boiling potatoes
2 cups chicken stock
1 cup water
1 onion
1 clove garlic
½ tsp. salt
2 tbsp. butter
1 cup half-and-half
1 cup cooked kale (about 8 leaves)

Peel the potatoes and simmer in the chicken stock and water. Chop the onion; mince the garlic clove and mash in the salt.

Sauté the onion with the garlic in the butter until wilted and add to the potatoes and stock. When the potatoes are tender (in about 1 hour), put the soup through a food mill or sieve and return to simmer. Add the half-and-half.

Meanwhile, wash the kale leaves. Cut off the thick lower portion of the center ribs. Cook the kale in boiling salted water for 20 minutes and drain. Cut the green leafy part from the fibrous center rib of each stalk. Chop the green part as fine as possible. The kale will now be reduced in amount to about half a cup. Immediately before serving, stir the chopped kale into the soup. Serves 6.

Curry Soup

Sari silks, tinkling elephant bells, self-realization shrines and mushroom-burger cafés are among India's gifts to the California scene. In the gourmet shops, curries, pappadums and cookbooks from Bombay find a ready market. Even a guru might approve of this golden soup. But if none is available, try it on your more exotic-minded friends.

½ medium onion
1 clove garlic
½ tsp. salt
3 tbsp. butter
1 tbsp. flour
½ apple
½ banana
½ tsp. curry powder
2 cups chicken stock
1 cup milk
½ cup unsweetened coconut milk
Dry sherry

Chop the onion, mash the garlic in salt, and sauté these in 1½ tablespoons butter until the onion is transparent. Sprinkle with the flour and cook until the flour is lightly browned.

Peel and chop the apple and sauté in the remaining butter in a separate pan. When the apple is tender, add the banana, sliced, and the curry powder. Cook until the banana is soft.

Add the onion and garlic and the apple-banana mixture to the chicken stock and simmer for ½ hour. Purée through a food mill or sieve. Add the milk and coconut milk. Test for seasoning and simmer another ½ hour.

To serve, place ½ teaspoon sherry in each bowl, then pour in the soup. Makes 6 first course servings.

Fresh Coconut Soup

Fresh, creamy coconut is irresistible eaten straight from the shell, shredded over fruit salads or sweetened and served as dessert. It can also be used to make this delicate, tropical soup.

1 cup shredded fresh coconut
2 cups milk
2 cups chicken stock
2 tbsp. sherry
½ tsp. salt
1½ tbsp. butter
1 tbsp. flour
¼ tsp. coconut extract
    Rum

Combine the coconut with 1 cup of milk in the blender and spin until the coconut is ground as fine as possible. Pour into the soup pan; rinse out the blender with the other cup of milk and add. Place coconut and milk over low heat and bring slowly to a boil. Then add the heated chicken stock, the sherry and the salt. If the stock is salty, you may need less seasoning.

In a small bowl, work the butter with the flour until well blended. Add a little soup gradually, stirring constantly, until the mixture is liquid and smooth. Stir this back into the soup. Bring the soup to a boil and keep at a low boil until slightly thickened.

Add the coconut extract. To serve, pour 1–2 teaspoons of rum in each bowl and add the soup. Serves 6.

NOTE: This soup should stand overnight to develop its flavor. The fine particles of coconut, which make the soup slightly crunchy, can be strained out if you prefer.

East First Street Suimono

Dashi, the basic Japanese soup stock, is a distinctively flavored, tea-colored broth made by steeping shaved katsuobushi (dried bonito) and kombu (dried kelp) with water and a little seasoning. If that sounds too complicated, do as the Japanese do. Buy the dashi ingredients packed in neat little bags to be dropped teabag style into boiling water.

In Los Angeles, East First Street is a good place to buy the dashi needed for the clear soup called "suimono." This suimono is made by pouring the boiling stock over tiny pieces of vegetables selected and shaped according to the artistry of the cook.

    1 packet instant dashi
    3 cups water
    1 carrot
    1 stalk of celery
    1 or 2 dried black Oriental mushrooms
    Sesame oil
    2 tsp. soy sauce
    Fresh ginger root

Boil the packet of instant dashi in the water for 5–7 minutes and discard like a teabag.

In each soup bowl, place 3 thin strips of carrot, 2 crosswise slices of celery, 2 pieces of chopped black mushroom (soften the mushrooms first in hot water), 2 drops of sesame oil and ⅓ teaspoon soy sauce. Put pieces of fresh ginger in a garlic press and squeeze a few drops of ginger juice into each bowl. Pour the boiling dashi over and serve. Makes 6 servings.

Tofu Vegetable Tapestry

Oriental vegetables weave a subtle tapestry in this soup, and the sesame oil, fresh ginger root, and black mushrooms give it the unmistakable perfume of the Far East. The tofu, or soy bean curd, provides a mild, smooth-textured note in the midst of the rich tapestry.

2 dried black Oriental mushrooms
¼ cup water chestnuts
2 green onion tops
¼ cup raw chicken
3 cups light chicken broth
½ tsp. salt
1 tsp. soy sauce
½ tsp. minced fresh ginger root
½ tsp. sesame oil
2 half-inch slices from a cake of tofu (soy bean curd)
4 whole spinach leaves

Soak the dried mushrooms in hot water until soft, then chop them. Slice the water chestnuts; chop the onion tops; and mince the chicken.

Bring the chicken broth to a boil. Add the mushrooms, water chestnuts, chicken, salt, soy sauce, ginger, and sesame oil. Simmer for ½ hour.

When ready to serve, bring the soup to a boil again and test for seasoning. Add more sesame oil and ginger if necessary. Their flavor should be distinct, but subtle.

Cut the tofu slices into ½-inch squares. Simmer in the soup until the tofu is heated through. Just before serving, add the onion tops and spinach leaves. Serves 4.

Batida de Papaya

Batidas are Puerto Rican fruit drinks—luscious, foamy blends of fresh fruit, flavorings, and ice. The method for making this batida came from a café in Old San Juan, the papayas from Hawaii. Thick as a milk shake and scented with the tropics, it makes an unusual first course that one can best describe as somewhere between a soup and a fruit cocktail.

    1 very ripe papaya
    2 tsp. fresh lime juice
    2 tsp. sugar
      Pinch of salt
    ¼ cup half-and-half
    2 tbsp. rum
    1 heaping cup cracked ice

Cut the papaya in half and scoop out the seeds. Slice the papaya into sections and peel. Place papaya in the blender with the rest of the ingredients and blend until smooth and thick. Turn the blender to high speed and then off several times to facilitate the blending.

Serve the batida in small glass bowls or in sherbet glasses, decorating the rims with a slice of lime. These proportions will make 2 large servings or 3 small ones.

Aunt Helen's Danish Buttermilk Soup

Soups can end a meal as well as begin one. And this Danish soup, from an old family recipe, forms a handsome finale with its snowy meringue topping and its tangy, surprising flavor. The tapioca thickens the soup until its texture is like a pudding.

    2 cups buttermilk
    ¼ cup sugar
    1 strip lemon peel
    1 cinnamon stick

Pinch of salt
⅓ cup seedless raisins
3 tbsp. minute tapioca
1 egg, separated, plus 1 egg white
¼ cup sugar for the meringue
2 tsp. orange Curaçao

Combine the buttermilk with 3 tablespoons sugar, the lemon peel, cinnamon stick, salt, raisins, and tapioca. Bring slowly to a boil, stirring constantly. Beat the egg yolk with 1 tablespoon sugar. Add a little of the soup gradually to the egg mixture to prevent curdling and combine the egg with the soup. Bring to a boil again. Remove from heat and cool slightly.

To make the meringue, beat the 2 egg whites until stiff; fold in ¼ cup sugar and the Curaçao. Divide the soup among 4 small bowls. Cover each with meringue and place under the broiler until the·meringue is browned. Makes 4 servings.

Almond-Peach Atole

Atole is the name for the sweetened corn gruel that you see being consumed in the market places of Mexico and Central America. The gruel is thickened with "masa," the corn dough used for making tortillas, or with cornstarch. It may be flavored with fruits, nuts or chocolate or with nothing other than the corn itself. In this recipe, fresh peaches, especially if on the tart side, contrast pleasingly with the sweetened, almond soup.

2 fresh peaches
½ cup blanched almonds
2¼ cups milk
⅓ cup sugar
1½ tsp. cornstarch
½ cup water
    Pinch of salt
¼ tsp. almond extract
1 egg
2 tbsp. rum

Peel the peaches; chop them coarsely and sprinkle with a little sugar; set aside. Place the almonds and ¾ cup milk in the blender and blend until the nuts are finely ground. Combine the rest of the milk with the sugar and the cornstarch, which has been dissolved in the water. Bring to a boil. Add the salt, almond extract, and ground nut mixture. Boil until slightly thickened. Cool. Beat the egg and add. Bring to a boil again. Add the chopped peaches to the soup only long enough to heat them. Stir in the rum and serve hot. Makes 4–6 servings.

3

Salads

You could call California a salad bowl as well as a melting pot. Our most prevalent form of exercise consists of tossing exorbitant mounds of greens with dressings of every conceivable sort. This culinary fixation is not hard to understand, for the makings of a great salad spring forth everywhere—from the bulging produce counters of our markets and from the soil, whether it be farmland, wild hillside, or vacant lot. Things like to grow here, and even a crack in the sidewalk will produce a crop that just might include a wild herb.

I know decorous ladies who, at the right time of year, park their cars near a certain hillside in Los Angeles and trespass blithely as they pluck wild fennel. And a lavender flowered plant that invaded my yard unfailingly attracts the Japanese who come to garden or keep house. They carry away handfuls, for it seems to be an important ingredient in their cookery, although none can tell me its name.

The warmth, freshness, and greenery of our environment inspire salad eating, and the craving for salads can be as relentless as thirst. On a trip up Highway 101, which pierces a good deal of crop country, I was entranced with the aroma of onions and garlic around King City. By the time I reached Salinas, greens were fairly floating through the air—a veritable agricultural smog. I wanted to capture them right then in a salad bowl—any salad bowl—but, unfortunately, motels don't seem to supply such conveniences.

It is amazing what can be done starting with lettuce and a basic oil-and-vinegar dressing. Our variations take in almost anything you can find in the supermarket—meat, cheese, bread, every type of vegetable and fruit, coconut, soy sauce, ginger root, eggs, anchovies, pinto beans, chiles, chili powder, nopales (cactus leaves), wine, rum, yogurt, nuts and even candy. Don't worry. Not all of these wind up in any one salad. We wouldn't eat it either.

Nevertheless, West Coast salads can be formidable. There are those who laugh at us for consuming prodigious platefuls before our main course. This order of serving, common in restaurants, has a certain advantage. If the meal that follows disappoints, you will be too full to care—and the salad is always good.

Those who call us barbaric are generally food snobs. Their ideal is the delicate helping of lettuce served in Europe as a palate cleanser after the main course. I have been to France and cleansed my palate on their salads. I found the lettuce superb and the dressings simple but perfectly seasoned. But there is more than one way to go, and out West our salads are important dishes in their own right, a featured part of the meal. Picture steak and baked potato without a tossed green salad. And what would a hearty, steaming platter of spaghetti be without its refreshing accompaniment of greens?

Some of our salads are truly gigantic. I saw one tossed in a handsome architectural pot big enough to hold a good-sized shrub. But there are also the dainty bits of vinegared vegetables that the Japanese set out on dishes tiny enough to come from a doll set.

The basic rules of salad making have been thoroughly preached by our culinary missionaries. So I will not linger over the routine of washing the greens, patting them gently with paper towels, tearing them into manageable pieces, and tossing them carefully with the dressing at the last minute.

I often drain my greens in a salad basket, that ingenious device of the French, who are never at a loss in handling food. But my salad basket comes from Mexico, and the one time I went outside to dry the greens by swinging the basket wildly in the French fashion, I lost my grip, and voila!—a fluttery downpour of lettuce.

My own rules for salad making include chilling the greens before tossing the salad and frosting the plates in the freezer.

The recipes that follow are low on the shivery, quivery molded salads that are the delight of cafeterias and tearooms, for I would rather control sweetness and flavor myself than rely on flavored gelatins. However, there is one exception in which guava nectar, rosé wine and fresh strawberries go to work on raspberry gelatin with notable results. And using unflavored gelatin, I came up with a sweet-sour wine mold that I think could stand up to a roast. I would not hesitate to serve it to the manliest of guests.

The remaining salads are made in many ways—torn, shredded, tossed, marinated and, in one case, doused with rum. Some are elaborate, huge, and colorfully garnished. Others are small and simple. You will find salads that are salty and pungent and a few that are downright sweet. In other words, there is something to harmonize with almost any dish you plan to serve and many ideas to please the palate that likes the adventure of something new.

Each salad is presented with its own dressing, but the dressing ingredients are, in most cases, set forth separately so that you can borrow them to toss with combinations of your own.

Tossed Garbanzo Bowl

The technique of marinating garbanzo beans employed in this salad is a handy one. The beans keep well, if stored in the refrigerator, and add taste and flair to a simple green salad tossed in a hurry.

1 (15-oz.) can garbanzo beans

GARBANZO MARINADE:
   2 tbsp. oil
   2 tbsp. cider vinegar
   ½ tsp. salt
   ¼ tsp. pepper

   1 head romaine
   2 tomatoes, cut in eighths
   ¼ cup chopped chives
   ¼ cup cilantro

THE DRESSING:
   6 tbsp. oil
   3 tbsp. cider vinegar
   1 clove garlic
   ½ tsp. salt
   ¼ tsp. pepper
   ¼ tsp. dry mustard
   ¼ tsp. fines herbes

Drain the garbanzo beans (the can will yield about 2 cups). Place the beans in a pint jar and add the oil, vinegar, salt, and pepper as listed under the marinade. Cover the jar, shake well and store in the refrigerator. Shake the jar occasionally.

To make the salad, wash the romaine, dry it thoroughly, and tear it in pieces. Place the romaine in a salad bowl. In the center, place 1 cup of the marinated garbanzo beans, reserving the rest for future use. Surround the beans with tomato wedges and sprinkle with chives and cilantro.

To make the dressing, combine the oil and vinegar in a small jar. Add the garlic, mashed in the salt, the pepper, mustard, and fines herbes. Shake well. Toss the salad with the dressing at the table. Makes 4–5 servings.

Ensalada de Cacahuates

Cacahuates are peanuts, and they make a great addition to a salad, as you will find if you try this unusual but simple combination of flavors. The Queso Enchilado is a crumbly, salty white cheese that the Mexicans like. If you can't get it, substitute packaged grated Parmesan cheese.

THE DRESSING: *Excellent*

1 clove garlic
1 tsp. salt
2 tsp. sugar
½ tsp. freshly ground black pepper
½ tsp. dry mustard
½ cup oil
¼ cup lemon juice

1 head red lettuce
1 onion
¼ cup dry-roasted peanuts — *Planter's Dry Roasted ONLY*
Queso Enchilado or packaged grated Parmesan cheese

Mash the garlic clove in the salt and place in a jar with the sugar, pepper, mustard, oil, and lemon juice. Shake well and chill.

Wash the lettuce and tear it into bite-size pieces. Slice the onion paper-thin and separate the slices into rings. Combine the lettuce and onions in a salad bowl. Separate the peanuts into halves and sprinkle them over the salad along with a generous amount of crumbled cheese. Shake the dressing thoroughly, pour over the salad, and toss. Makes 6 servings.

Sharon's Salad with Green Goddess Dressing

Your guests will be impressed when you bring in this colorful salad with its carefully arranged pattern of contrasting vegetables. It's a hearty salad with that little touch of artistry which makes the difference between an ordinary dish and a memorable one.

1 carrot
Bottled French or Italian dressing
½ medium cauliflower
2 tomatoes
1 head romaine

GREEN GODDESS DRESSING:

1 egg
½ tsp. salt
¼ tsp. dry mustard
3 tbsp. sherry wine vinegar or other wine vinegar
½ cup oil
1 clove garlic
½ tsp. anchovy paste
¼ tsp. freshly ground black pepper
1 heaping tbsp. minced parsley
Pinch of cumin
¼ tsp. chervil
3 tbsp. cream
2 tbsp. chopped chives

Scrape the carrot, cut it into julienne strips, and parboil the strips 5 minutes in salted water. Drain the strips, toss them with a little French dressing, and chill.

Break the cauliflower into flowerets. Slice the flowerets if they are very large and parboil them in salted water 3 minutes. Drain, marinate in French dressing, and chill separately from the carrots.

Cut the tomatoes into eighths and chill. Wash and pat dry the romaine, tear it into bite-size pieces, and chill.

To make the dressing, place the egg, salt, and mustard in the blender and whirl until smooth. Add 1 tablespoon of the vinegar and blend again. With the blender at full speed, add the oil by droplets, thus forming mayonnaise. Now add the garlic clove, anchovy paste, pepper, parsley, cumin, chervil, cream, and the remaining 2 tablespoons vinegar and blend thoroughly. Chill until serving time.

In a salad bowl, make a bed of the romaine. Place the drained carrots in the center. Surround them with the drained cauliflowerets. Make a circle of tomato wedges around the cauliflower and, if the bowl is large, another circle of tomato wedges around the edge of the bowl. Sprinkle the vegetables with the chopped chives.

Bring the dressing to the table in a separate container, pour it over the salad, toss and serve. Makes about 5 servings.

California Chopped Salad

good, ~~noneed~~ to cook Cauliflower

This salad once ruined a dinner party. While the guests enjoyed themselves after dinner, I had to write out copies of the recipe!

1½ cups coarsely chopped cauliflower
1 cup canned kidney beans
2 green onions, chopped
1 tbsp. chopped green chile

THE DRESSING:
¼ cup oil
2 tbsp. vinegar
1 clove garlic
½ tsp. salt
¼ tsp. freshly ground black pepper
¼ tsp. sugar
⅛ tsp. cumin

1 tomato, peeled, seeded, and chopped
4 lettuce leaves

Parboil the cauliflower in salted water for 1 minute. Drain and rinse with cold water. Combine the cauliflower, kidney beans, onions, and chile in a bowl.

Combine the oil and vinegar in a small jar. Add the garlic, mashed in the salt, the pepper, sugar, and cumin. Shake thoroughly. Pour the dressing over the vegetables and toss carefully with a fork. Cover the salad and chill. Add the chopped tomato just before serving. Toss the salad again lightly and place a mound of vegetables on each lettuce leaf. Makes 4 servings.

Mexican Flag Salad

The red, white, and green of the Mexican flag are repeated in the vegetables that decorate this salad.

THE DRESSING:
    6 tbsp. oil
    3 tbsp. red wine vinegar
    1 tbsp. red wine
    1 clove garlic
    ½ tsp. salt
    ¼ tsp. freshly ground black pepper
    ¼ tsp. salad herbs
    ½ tsp. patis (liquefied anchovy)

    1 zucchini
        Bottled French or Italian dressing
    1 small onion
    2 tomatoes
    1 head romaine or red lettuce
    2–3 tbsp. crumbled Queso Enchilado or packaged grated
        Parmesan cheese

Make the dressing several hours before you prepare the salad so the flavors can blend. In a jar combine the oil, vinegar, wine, the garlic clove mashed in the salt, the pepper, herbs, and anchovy liquid. Shake well.

Parboil the zucchini 5 minutes. Drain and slice very thin. Marinate the zucchini slices in a small amount of the bottled French dressing. Or make your own marinade using 1 part vinegar to 2 parts oil with salt and pepper to taste. Chill the zucchini.

Slice the onion into paper-thin rings and cut the rings in half. Cut the tomatoes into eighths.

Wash the romaine and tear it into bite-size pieces. Make a bed of romaine in a salad bowl. On top arrange the vegetables to represent the red, white, and green of the Mexican flag. Place the tomatoes in the center. Circle them with onion, then add a ring of zucchini slices. If desired, add another circle of tomato wedges around the zucchini. Sprinkle the cheese over the salad. Pour the dressing over and toss at the table. Makes 4–6 servings.

Cucumber Tomato Spread

If you're tired of the inevitable tossed green salad, try this.

½ medium cucumber
2 tbsp. grated onion
¼ cup sour cream
2 tbsp. mayonnaise
1 tbsp. cider vinegar
1 small clove garlic
½ tsp. salt
½ tsp. chopped parsley
⅛ tsp. dill weed
1 tsp. sugar
¼ tsp. freshly ground black pepper
2 tomatoes

Excellent sauce and pretty

Peel the cucumber, cut it in half lengthwise, and scoop out the seeds. Grate the cucumber and drain off the liquid it produces. Drain the grated onion. Blend the onion and cucumber with the sour cream, mayonnaise, and vinegar. Mince the garlic and mash it in the salt. Add the garlic to the cucumber mixture along with the parsley, dill, sugar, and pepper. Stir thoroughly. Cover and refrigerate overnight.

Peel the tomatoes and chill them. When ready to serve, slice the tomatoes and spread the slices thickly with the cucumber dressing. Makes 4 servings.

Caesar Salad Boccaccio

One of my favorite restaurants is in California, but not in the United States. Here's the answer to the riddle: it is a place called Boccaccio's Nuevo Marianna on the outskirts of Tijuana in Baja California. When you order dinner, they wheel a cart to the table and, before your eyes, toss a beautiful Caesar salad. If you watch carefully, as I did, you might come up with this recipe.

1 or 2 cloves garlic
⅓ cup oil
1 head romaine
Juice of 1 lemon
1 egg
Few drops of Worcestershire sauce
Scant ½ tsp. salt
Freshly ground black pepper
½ cup or more freshly grated Parmesan cheese

Several hours or the day before preparing the salad, combine the garlic cloves and oil in a jar and cover tightly.

Wash and tear up enough of the romaine for 4 people and place in a large salad bowl. At the table (you should make quite a production of this), pour the oil into the bowl, discarding the garlic. Squeeze in the lemon juice, break in the egg and add the Worcestershire sauce. Tilt the bowl and beat the egg and other dressing ingredients together. Now add the salt, plenty of pepper and about ⅓ cup cheese. Toss the salad and serve with more cheese sprinkled over each serving. Makes 4 servings.

Anchovy Pepper Salad

This savory little antipasto goes as well with steak as with spaghetti.

1 green pepper
4 large stalks celery

THE DRESSING:

2 tbsp. lemon juice
1 tbsp. vinegar
6 tbsp. oil
½ tsp. salt
¼ tsp. freshly ground black pepper
¼ tsp. paprika

4 lettuce leaves
8 anchovy fillets

2 tomatoes, cut into wedges
Ripe olives

Remove the stem and seeds of the pepper and slice it in thin strips. Cut the celery stalks into 2-inch sections and the sections into 4 or more sticks. Combine the lemon juice, vinegar, oil, salt, pepper, and paprika in a jar and shake thoroughly. Pour the dressing over the celery and green pepper and chill, stirring occasionally.

To serve, place a lettuce leaf on each plate. On a corner of the leaf place a mound of the marinated vegetables and top each mound with 2 crisscrossed anchovy fillets. Arrange tomato wedges around the mound and garnish with an olive or two. Makes 4 servings.

Longan Cucumber Relish

If you're serving spicy foods, the crisp, chilled cucumbers and gently flavored longans featured in this salad will provide a cooling contrast. It's a trick I learned in Southeast Asia. Try it the next time you serve curry.

1 medium cucumber
1 medium carrot
1 cup drained longans

THE DRESSING:

3 tbsp. juice from canned longans
1 tbsp. pon vinegar
1 tsp. lime juice
2 tsp. oil
   Pinch of grated lime peel
1 small piece fresh ginger root

Peel the cucumber, cut it in half lengthwise, and scrape out the seeds. Cut the cucumber halves into strips, then into dice. Scrape the carrot and cut it in julienne strips. Drop the carrot strips in boiling water and parboil 1 minute. Drain and rinse with cold water.

Place the diced cucumber, the carrot strips and longans in a bowl. Blend the longan juice, pon vinegar, lime juice, and oil and pour over the salad. Add the lime peel. Using a garlic press, squeeze a few drops of ginger root juice over the salad. Cover and chill, stirring occasionally. Makes 4 servings.

Sweet-Sour Wine Mold

Chinese and Polynesian cooks dreamed up the sweet-sour flavorings that combine with wine in this deep-toned mold. It is one of the few gelatin salads that I would serve with steak or roast beef, and I have added enough gelatin so that it won't melt as you eat it.

1½ cups dry red wine
6 tbsp. sugar
1 small stick cinnamon
1 clove
1 strip orange peel
1 strip lemon peel
2 env. unflavored gelatin
1½ cups pineapple juice
1 tbsp. cider vinegar
1 cup pineapple chunks, drained
½ cup sliced celery
¼ cup diced green pepper

THE DRESSING:
1 cup mayonnaise
½ tsp. grated orange peel
½ tsp. grated lemon peel
½ tsp. grated lime peel

Place the wine in a saucepan with the sugar, cinnamon stick, clove, and orange and lemon peel. The strips of peel should not include any of the white portion. Bring the wine to a boil and stir until the sugar is dissolved. Remove from heat, cover, and let steep for 1 hour.

Soften the gelatin in ½ cup pineapple juice. Bring the remaining 1 cup pineapple juice to a boil, add the gelatin mixture and stir until dissolved. Strain the wine into the pineapple juice, removing the peels, cinnamon stick, and clove. Add the vinegar. Cool first, then chill until the mixture begins to set. Fold in the pineapple, celery, and green pepper, turn into a 1½-quart mold and chill until firm.

To make the dressing, blend the mayonnaise with the grated orange, lemon, and lime peel and chill for 1–2 hours to let the flavors mellow.

Dip the mold briefly into hot water and turn the salad out onto a serving platter. Accompany with the flavored mayonnaise. Makes 6 servings.

Cucumber Sunomono

Sunomono is a Japanese salad with a vinegar dressing. This version adds sesame oil and ginger juice for a special flavor.

Medium

1 cucumber
1 tsp. salt
10 water chestnuts
2 large green onions

THE DRESSING:

1½ tbsp. rice wine vinegar
½ tsp. sesame oil
½ tsp. sugar
¼ tsp. salt
1 small piece ginger root
Toasted sesame seeds
Soy sauce (optional)

Peel the cucumber and cut it in half lengthwise. Scoop out the seeds. Slice the cucumber paper thin and sprinkle with 1 tsp. salt. After 20 minutes, pour off the liquid that has accumulated and squeeze the slices by handfuls to remove as much liquid as possible.

Slice the water chestnuts paper thin and chop the onions. Mix the vegetables with the rice wine vinegar, sesame oil, sugar, and ¼ teaspoon salt. Using a garlic press, squeeze a few drops of ginger root juice into the salad. Mix thoroughly and chill. Serve in small mounds sprinkled with toasted sesame seeds. Soy sauce may be added at the table, if desired. Makes 4 servings.

Chilled Dilled Lima Beans

The lima bean is underrated as a salad vegetable but does a beautiful job if given a chance. This recipe has a special twist. Stop half way and you have a savory hot vegetable, continue and you have an unusual salad or cold vegetable relish.

1 (10-oz.) pkg. frozen lima beans
1 small onion
1 small clove garlic
½ tsp. salt
¾ cup water

THE DRESSING:
6 tbsp. oil
2 tbsp. vinegar
½ tsp. dill weed
¼ tsp. salt
Lettuce leaves

Place the lima beans in a saucepan. Add the onion, sliced paper thin, the garlic, mashed in the salt, and the water. Cover and bring to a boil, then reduce the heat and simmer, loosely covered, for 10–15 minutes. The beans should be tender but not mushy. At this point, you can drain the beans and serve them as a hot vegetable. Otherwise, cool the beans. Combine the oil, vinegar, dill, and salt in a pint jar and shake thoroughly. Add the beans to the jar, cover tightly and turn the jar back and forth a few times to distribute the dressing. Refrigerate overnight. Turn the jar occasionally to marinate the beans thoroughly. Serve in small ramekins lined with a portion of lettuce leaf. Makes 4 servings.

Street Vendors' Salad

If you've ever been in Mexico, you can't have missed the street vendors with their carts of appetizing fare including crisp, white slices of "jicama" sprinkled with chili powder. In Guatemala, I bought orange slices dusted with chili powder from a charming urchin, who attracted throngs while he peeled the oranges with an impressive machine. It's not hard to find jicamas in Los Angeles—if you know where to look—and since we're famous for oranges, I combine the two in this version of the street vendors' wares. In a pinch you could substitute cucumber for the jicama, which is a crisp, bulbous root vegetable covered with a thin brown skin.

1 orange
½ cup diced jicama or cucumber

THE DRESSING:
3 tbsp. oil
1½ tbsp. wine vinegar
¼ tsp. salt
Dash pepper
¼ tsp. hot pepper sauce

½ onion
¼ cup walnuts (optional)
3 lettuce leaves
Chili powder

Peel the orange and slice it in thin cartwheels. Marinate the orange and jicama in a dressing made with the oil and vinegar, salt, pepper, and hot pepper sauce. Chill. Just before serving, slice the onion paper thin and coarsely chop the walnuts. Toss the onion and walnuts with the orange slices, the jicama, and their dressing. Line each plate with a large lettuce leaf and place a helping of the salad on the leaf. Dust lightly with chili powder. Makes 3 servings.

Greens with Lemon Dressing

Take your choice of greens for this salad. I like to combine two or more varieties, for example, butter lettuce with romaine or romaine with watercress.

Enough salad greens for 4 servings

THE DRESSING:

Excellent Dressing

3 tbsp. lemon juice
7 tbsp. oil
2 cloves garlic
¾ tsp. salt
2 tbsp. grated onion
¼ tsp. lemon pepper marinade
⅛ tsp. cumin
1 tsp. sugar
¼ tsp. tarragon

Combine the lemon juice and oil in a jar. Add the garlic cloves, mashed in the salt; the onion and its liquid, the lemon pepper marinade, cumin, and sugar. Crumble in the tarragon. Cover and shake well. Let stand to mellow. Shake thoroughly before using and toss with the greens. Makes 4 servings.

Middle East Medley

Yogurt and mint are mainstays of the Middle East, but the mint in my garden came from the Middle West—Dubuque, Iowa, to be exact. Nevertheless, it adds an appropriately eastern flavor to this salad, which was inspired by one of my Armenian friends.

THE DRESSING:
½ cup oil
¼ cup red wine vinegar
½ tsp. or more salt
1 clove garlic

2 medium tomatoes
1 medium cucumber
1 medium onion
2 green onions
1 small green pepper
1 tsp. chopped fresh mint
5–6 cups torn lettuce
¼ cup yogurt
    Freshly ground black pepper
16 pitted ripe olives

Combine the oil, vinegar, salt, and garlic. If you like lots of garlic, mince it and mash it in the salt before adding it to the dressing; otherwise add the clove whole and remove it later. Shake the dressing thoroughly and let stand for several hours.

Chill the vegetables before preparing the salad. Peel the tomatoes and cut them into eighths. Peel the cucumber and cut it into thin slices. Slice the onion into paper thin rings. Chop the green onions. Cut the pepper into strips. Combine the vegetables and the mint in a salad bowl. Toss thoroughly with the dressing.

Make a bed of lettuce on each salad plate and place on it a generous helping of the vegetables. In the center, place a dollop of yogurt, sprinkled thickly with freshly ground pepper. Garnish each salad with 4 olives. Makes 4 servings.

One-Bean Salad

If you're bored with the tried-and-true three-bean salads, try this for a change. The one bean is the pinto, which is fundamental to Mexican cookery. Nopales are tender portions of cactus that are sold fresh or canned in little green dice in Mexican markets. I use canned nopales for this salad.

1 (15-oz.) can pinto beans
1 small onion
½ cup canned nopales, drained

THE DRESSING:

6 tbsp. oil
3 tbsp. vinegar
1 clove garlic
½ tsp. salt
¼ tsp. cumin
¼ tsp. oregano
¼ tsp. freshly ground black pepper
    Dash of cayenne

    Lettuce leaves
    Toasted tortilla chips

Drain and rinse the beans. Slice the onion paper thin and separate the slices into rings. Combine the beans, onion rings, and nopales in a bowl. In a small jar, combine the oil and vinegar, the garlic, mashed in the salt, the cumin, oregano, pepper, and cayenne. Cover the jar and shake until the dressing is well blended. Toss the vegetables with the dressing. Cover and chill, stirring occasionally. Mound each serving on a lettuce leaf and garnish with a tortilla chip. Makes 3 servings.

Wilted Spinach Salad

The dressing that wilts the spinach should be sweet, sharp, and pungent. I always taste it to make sure the seasonings are right. If guests are coming, you can prepare the dressing in advance, then bring it to a boil at serving time.

1 large bunch spinach
4 slices bacon
⅓ cup cider vinegar
5 tsp. sugar
¼ tsp. powdered lemon grass (optional)
½ tsp. dry mustard

¼ tsp. garlic powder
    Dash of cayenne
½ tsp. salt
¼ tsp. freshly ground black pepper

Wash the spinach, drain it thoroughly, and pat dry with paper towels. Place the spinach in a salad bowl.

Fry the bacon until crisp and drain. Let the drippings cool slightly in the pan. Add the vinegar, sugar, lemon grass, mustard, garlic powder, cayenne, salt, and pepper. Stir and taste for seasoning.

Crumble the bacon and sprinkle it over the spinach. Bring the dressing to a full boil, pour it over the salad and toss. Makes 4 servings.

Fresno Tossed Salad with Yogurt Dressing

Many Armenians have settled in California, particularly in Fresno, where they have become prosperous growers. Where you find Armenians you also find yogurt, and a little of it has made its way into this salad, which was designed to cool off hot summer days in the San Joaquin Valley.

THE DRESSING:
    2 tbsp. yogurt
    2 tbsp. wine vinegar
    ½ cup oil
    2 tbsp. grated onion
    1 large clove garlic
    ½ tsp. salt
    1 tsp. sugar
    Pinch of dill weed

    Romaine
    ½ medium cucumber

Make the dressing the day before you serve the salad. Combine the yogurt, vinegar, oil, and onion in a jar. Add the garlic, mashed in the salt, the sugar, and the dill. Mix the dressing thoroughly and chill.

Wash and tear up enough romaine for 4 people. Peel the cucumber and slice very thin. Chill the romaine and cucumber. To serve, place the greens and cucumber in a salad bowl and toss with enough of the dressing to coat them thoroughly. Makes 4 servings.

Vinegared Vegetables

Savoy cabbage gives this Japanese-style salad a prettier color and milder flavor than other cabbage. To make the small amount of dashi called for, I tear open a packet of instant dashi, measure out ½ teaspoon, bring it to a boil with 3 tablespoons of water, and immediately strain the broth through a very fine sieve. The daikon is a large, mild radish that one sees everywhere in Japan. It grows in California too.

THE DRESSING:

3 tbsp. dashi
3 tbsp. rice wine vinegar
1 tbsp. oil
½ tsp. salt
½ tsp. sugar
Dash of garlic powder
Dash of monosodium glutamate

2½–3 cups shredded Savoy cabbage
¼ cup chopped green onions
¼ cup grated daikon

Combine the dashi, vinegar, oil, salt, sugar, garlic powder, and monosodium glutamate and shake thoroughly. In a salad bowl, place the shredded cabbage and the onions. Measure the grated daikon and press out a little of its liquid, then add to the salad. Toss the salad with the dressing and chill 2 hours. Makes 4 servings.

Manila Salad

The pretty, flower-like women of the Philippines add an exotic note to Los Angeles. From them came the idea for this tropical salad.

6 canned pineapple rings
2 avocados

GINGER MAYONNAISE DRESSING:
½ cup mayonnaise
1½ tbsp. ginger syrup
1 tsp. cream sherry

¼ cup toasted almonds, chopped
6 lettuce leaves
Shredded coconut
3 maraschino cherries, halved

Drain the pineapple rings and cut them into small chunks. Peel the avocados, slice them, and cube the slices. Blend the mayonnaise with the syrup and sherry. Combine the almonds, avocado, and pineapple and toss very gently with the dressing. Chill. To serve, place a portion of the salad on a lettuce leaf, sprinkle with coconut, and place a cherry half in the center. Makes 6 servings.

Pineapple-Daiquiri Fruit Cup

If guests are late and miss the cocktail hour, they'll feel relieved if you start the dinner with this spirited fruit cup. It also makes a good dessert.

Fresh pineapple
Limes
Powdered sugar
Rum
Mint sprigs

Slice and peel the pineapple, cut it in small chunks and chill. For each serving, take a stemmed sherbet or large cocktail glass, rub the rim with a cut lime and dip in powdered sugar to coat the rim. Fill each glass with chilled pineapple chunks.

Make daiquiris, allowing 1½ ounces of rum, the juice of ½ lime and 1 teaspoon powdered sugar to each drink. Divide each daiquiri between 2 servings of pineapple and decorate the servings with a mint sprig that has been dipped in powdered sugar.

Strawberry-Guava Salad

Here at last is a sweet gelatin salad that is not insipid. The guava nectar hints at the aromatic pungency of tropical fruit markets, and the brandy does wonders with the dressing.

    1 (12-oz.) can guava nectar
    1 (3-oz.) pkg. raspberry gelatin
    ½ cup rosé wine
    1 heaping cup fresh strawberries

THE DRESSING:
    2 (3-oz.) pkg. cream cheese, softened
    ¼ cup sour cream
    ¼ cup brandy
    2 tbsp. powdered sugar
    6 whole strawberries for garnish

Bring 1 cup guava nectar to a boil and pour it over the gelatin, stirring until the gelatin dissolves. Add the remaining ½ cup guava nectar and the wine. Cool, then chill until the mixture begins to set. Meanwhile, hull and slice the strawberries. Stir the berries into the setting gelatin and chill until firm.

To make the dressing, beat the cream cheese with the sour cream, stir in the brandy and sugar and chill thoroughly. Top each serving with a spoonful of dressing and garnish with a strawberry. Makes 6 servings.

Tahini Cabbage

A girl from Cairo introduced me to tahini, a soft paste made from crushed sesame seeds which adds nutty flavor to such varied fare as dips, fish, coffee cakes, cookies, and this salad. Don't use hommos tahini, which contains garbanzo beans, with this recipe. The sesame candy used as a topping comes in small thin squares and is sold in regular candy stores as well as Middle Eastern markets.

TAHINI DRESSING:
- ½ cup mayonnaise
- 2 tbsp. tahini
- 1 tbsp. honey
- ⅛ tsp. ground ginger

- 4 heaping cups finely shredded cabbage
  (about ½ medium cabbage)
- ½ cup shredded pineapple, drained
- 4 squares sesame brittle or toasted sesame seeds

Blend the mayonnaise with the tahini, honey, and ginger, and chill.

To shred the cabbage, cut it into quarters, cut out the core and slice paper thin beginning at the tip of each wedge. Discard the tough parts. Combine the cabbage and pineapple in a salad bowl and toss with the dressing.

Place the sesame brittle between sheets of waxed paper and crush with a rolling pin. Sprinkle the crumbs over each serving. If you prefer a less sweet salad, use the sesame seeds instead. Makes 4 servings.

Crunchy Pear Salad

This recipe stems from my salad days at Stanford University, where it was served at Lagunita Hall. Oddly enough, the grape-nuts taste like crunchy candy and not cereal when combined with the pear and mayonnaise.

Canned pear halves
Shredded lettuce
Mayonnaise
Cream
Grape-nuts

Ordinary —
the grape-nuts taste
like grape-nuts only
mushy.

Place each pear half on a bed of lettuce and spread with mayonnaise thinned with a little cream. Sprinkle generously with grape-nuts. Allow 1 pear half for each serving.

Papaya Cream Dressing

Papayas are not only a treat in themselves but make a delicious dressing for other fruit.

½ **ripe papaya**
½ **cup mayonnaise**
1 **tbsp. honey**
1 **tbsp. chopped candied ginger**

Cut the papaya half into strips, peel them and place them in the blender. Add the mayonnaise, honey, and ginger. Blend until smooth and creamy. Chill the dressing and serve it over pears, pineapple, or other fresh or canned fruit. Makes about 1 cup dressing.

4

Vegetables and Rice

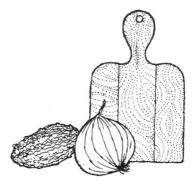

VEGETABLES

Vegetables are the underdogs of the cookery world, but they are pure gold in California. They proved more profitable than metallic ore to some of those swept here by the Gold Rush of 1849. Not everyone struck the dreamed-of vein or found the right glint in his pan. But all had to eat. And those who prospected in agriculture found spectacular rewards. An exhibit held in San Francisco in 1851 featured a beet weighing forty-seven pounds, a head of cabbage seven feet in circumference and other wonders from the soil. Far from a flash-in-the-pan, these outsized nuggets forecast a rich future in agriculture. Today California is the top farming state in the nation, a position based on the dollar value of our crops.

But the real start of agriculture in California goes back some eighty years before the prospectors. In 1769 Spain dispatched the first expeditions to settle Alta California. Two groups came by land and two by sea. Father Junípero Serra, who founded our missions, arrived with a land expedition from Baja California and broke ground for Mission San Diego de Alcalá July 16, 1769.

These expeditions came laden with foodstuffs, most of which spoiled on the way. Rice, wheat, millet, and orchard materials were brought for sowing. But plans went astray in the face of unexpectedly rugged reality. Conditions became so desperate and supplies so scarce that Father Serra gave up and prepared to return to Baja California. Fortunately, new supplies arrived to meet his deadline. In the next few years the missions gained a foothold and began to produce their crops.

Early Californians harvested quelites (wild greens), learned about cacomites (wild onions) from the Indians and grew chiles in abundance. Olive trees provided plenty of fruit, and the oil was used in cooking instead of butter. The potato arrived in 1786, but rice proved more acceptable to Spanish tastes.

Corn, beans, squash, tomatoes, and nopales (cactus leaves) were staples. To season the dishes one could pick wild herbs such as yerba buena, which is a type of mint, wild fennel, wild marjoram (oregano), basil, and rosemary.

Today the land produces an incredible diversity of crops. The vegetables appealing to Spaniards and Mexicans have made room for those used in Oriental cooking—daikons, lotus root, bok choy, Chinese broccoli, winter melon, burdock, bean sprouts, taro, and many others. The Chinese not only contributed their vegetables, but taught us to cook them until barely tender. This technique alone is enough to transform many a vegetable.

While our great agricultural valleys are thriving, the farmland that used to reach into our cities is disappearing under subdivisions. You have to go farther and farther from Los Angeles to find orange groves. But if you can spare a glance while hurtling along some freeway, you will see crops sprouting in the right of way. And a twenty-minute drive by freeway from the heart of Los Angeles will take you to fields where you can still buy sugary, tender fresh corn.

Someday I'd like a plot of land where I could experiment with vegetables. Once I had dinner with winemaker Joseph Heitz and his family at their home in the Napa Valley. I'll never forget the onions pulled straight from the soil to be simmered in his own Johannisberg Riesling.

At present my crops are limited to shallots, herbs, and hopefully, chayotes. With an agricultural tome published some fifty years ago in San Francisco as a guide, I planted two chayotes. But the promised gigantic vines never appeared. Neither has the tiniest sprout. So I discussed the matter with a fellow farmer who presides over a stall in Los Angeles' busy Grand Central Market. He said I should have both male and female chayotes. Since I'm naïve about such goings on in the vegetable world, I compromised and bought a chayote that had already sprouted.

Meanwhile, my herbs flourish wildly. Every summer I plant basil in order to make quantities of pesto, that Italian seasoning of pounded garlic, basil, and olive oil that you toss with steaming strands of spaghetti, butter, and Parmesan cheese. This year I have added lemon grass, which is essential for Indonesian, Thai, and Malayan dishes. I like lemon balm as a garnish for drinks, rose geranium as a flavoring for apple jelly. And I no longer need to pass by recipes that demand fresh thyme, tarragon, marjoram, rosemary, fennel, dill, sage, mint, chives, oregano, and—would you believe—burnet.

It is hard for me to understand why, in most of the nation, vegetables have been not only neglected but destroyed by well-meaning cooks. For years they have turned up as poor relations to the meat course, served out of a sense of duty and because, as mothers, school teachers, and Popeye insist, they are good for you. What else but duty would inspire one to eat the boiled and boring little clumps of green, orange, or yellow that one so frequently encounters.

You'll find these noxious dishes in California too, for many of our residents have come from other areas and are still steeped in bad habits. But native Californians have worked with vegetables for years. We know that the cook who treats them with respect easily earns a fabulous reputation. The guest who tastes a vegetable that is not only good but exciting is sure to stop in mid-mouthful and exclaim over it, so rare is the experience.

Pouring over California cookbooks dating back half a century or more, I find exotic concoctions like mashed potatoes whipped with coconut milk, dried bean croquettes with spinach sauce, rice cooked with saffron syrup, tomato sherbet, and a topping for vegetables that includes four kinds of liqueur, powdered sugar, cloves, and orange rind.

As for this last recipe, it is a mistake to think of "gourmet cooking" as complicated work requiring squads of expensive seasonings, wines and liqueurs.

The simplest cooking is often the best. When you have such superb vegetables as asparagus, tender broccoli, or sweet new carrots, you enhance their natural flavor rather than disguise it. This may take only a pinch of herbs, a hint of garlic, a little sugar, or wine, depending upon the vegetable.

In this chapter you will find no recipes for artichokes, although they are grown commercially only in California and are one of our great delicacies. Why? Because to me an artichoke is at its best when simmered in salted water until tender and then served hot with melted butter in which to dip the leaves. You don't need a recipe for that. And I have no patience with fussy recipes that stuff the artichokes with complex preparations, snip their leaves or cut out their hearts to be used as receptacles for other vegetables. That is cruelty indeed!

I say the best course is to leave a good thing as it is. That is why most of the recipes that follow are quite simple. In addition to the vegetables, you will find an interloping recipe for papaya, which is a fruit. And the chapter ends with a small section on one of my favorite activities, rice cookery.

Carrots

If you've hated carrots all your life, these California recipes will change your mind. The herbed carrots emigrated from Spain, the sesame carrots from Korea, and the drunken carrots show what our wine industry can do for a neglected vegetable. One trick: Cut carrots in sticks to blot out the memory of the usual sickly boiled rounds.

Herb Baked Carrots

5 medium carrots
1 small onion
2 tbsp. butter
3 tbsp. white wine
2 tbsp. water
Sprig of fresh thyme, oregano or other herb
Salt
1½ tbsp. almonds, blanched and chopped or ground
1 clove garlic, minced
½ tsp. chopped shallot (optional)
Pinch of cumin
Very small pinch of saffron
Chopped parsley

Cut the carrots in strips and chop the onion. Place the butter in a casserole and set in a 350° oven to melt. Now add the carrots and onion to the casserole with the wine, water, and herb sprig or an herb bouquet. Sprinkle with salt to taste, cover and return to the oven.

In a mortar mash together the almonds, garlic, shallot, cumin, and saffron. Dilute the resulting paste with a little additional white wine and pour this over the carrots.

Stir the carrots occasionally while baking. Bake, covered, until most of the liquid is absorbed and the carrots are tender, about 1 hour. Garnish each serving with a sprinkling of chopped parsley. Makes 4–5 servings.

Sesame Carrots

The sesame oil called for in this recipe is the Oriental type, which adds a delightful nutty flavor to the carrots.

4 carrots
2 tbsp. butter
1 tsp. sugar
¼ tsp. salt
½ tsp. sesame oil
1 tbsp. toasted sesame seeds

Cut the carrots in strips. Boil them in salted water for 10 minutes and drain. Melt the butter in a skillet. Add the carrots and sprinkle them with sugar and salt. Cook the carrots until tender and coated with butter. Then sprinkle with the sesame oil and sesame seeds. Toss to mix thoroughly and serve. Makes 4 servings.

Carrots Borracho
(*Drunken Carrots*)   Too subtle for me

Angelica, which is one of the oldest California wines, was a specialty of the missions and haciendas. It is still available, but any sweet wine may be used with this recipe.

½ cup angelica or other sweet white wine
¾ tsp. grated orange peel
2 tbsp. butter
¾ tsp. sugar
¾ tsp. salt
4 cups shredded carrots (about 3 large carrots)
4 tsp. orange Curaçao
Chopped toasted almonds

Combine the angelica, orange peel, butter, sugar, and salt in a saucepan and heat gently until the butter melts. Add the carrots and cook, covered, until the carrots are tender and most of the liquid is absorbed, about 20–25 minutes. Stir in the Curaçao and serve immediately sprinkled with chopped almonds. Makes 4 servings.

Chayotes

Sometimes smooth and sometimes bristling with spines, the chayote contains tender, delicate flesh that combines well with meat, seafood, and other vegetables. Chayotes flourish in California, and we also bring them up from Mexico. They are, I think, the most elegant of squash.

Chayotes Stuffed with Spinach

2 chayotes
1 small onion
1 clove garlic
Salt
1 tbsp. butter
⅓ cup cooked, chopped spinach
⅓–½ cup buttered bread crumbs

Very good

may do ahead & refrigerate

Cut the chayotes in half lengthwise and remove the seeds. Cook them in boiling salted water 20–30 minutes or until tender. Drain and scoop out the pulp, leaving the shells intact, and mash the pulp coarsely with a potato masher. Chop the onion. Mince the garlic and mash it in a little salt. Melt the butter in a skillet, add the onion and garlic and cook until the onion is tender but not browned. Add the spinach and the chayote pulp. Season with salt to taste and stir until blended. Fill the chayote shells with this mixture. Top with buttered bread crumbs and bake at 350° for 15 minutes, or until heated through. Makes 4 servings.

Chayotes with Bacon

2 large chayotes
4 slices bacon
1 small onion
2 tbsp. butter
Salt
Pepper

Okay – good

Cut the chayotes in half lengthwise and remove the seeds. Cook the chayotes in boiling salted water until tender, about 20–30 minutes. Drain. When the chayotes are cool enough to handle, peel and cube them. Fry the bacon until crisp, then drain and crumble it. Chop the onion. Melt the butter in a skillet, add the onion and cook it until tender but not browned. Add the cubed chayotes and season with salt and pepper to taste. Toss with the crumbled bacon and cook only until heated through. Makes 6 servings.

Silverado Beans

The Silverado Trail was a stagecoach route running through the Napa Valley in what is today premium California wine country. Robert Louis Stevenson wrote about the area in his "The Silverado Squatters," and the Chinese came there to work the vineyards. This colorful country is reflected in the following casserole that borrows wine from the vineyards, sausages from the Chinese, and beans from the packs of the adventurers who roamed the trail. The trail is still there, by the way, conveniently paved for a drive through some of the loveliest country in California.

    2 cups dried navy beans
    3 Chinese sausages
    1 large onion, sliced
    1 bay leaf
 1½ tsp. salt
    1 clove garlic
   ¼ tsp. cumin
   ¼ tsp. coarse black pepper
 1¼ cups Burgundy wine
 1½ cups bean stock

Cover the beans with hot water and soak overnight. The next morning, drain the beans, cover them again with hot water, and bring to a boil. Simmer until the skin breaks when you blow on a bean. Meanwhile, wash the sausages and steam them for 30 minutes. Cut them into ⅜-inch slices. In a large casserole, make a layer of onion slices, then a layer of sausage slices. Add the bay leaf and all the beans, lifting them from their cooking liquid with a slotted spoon. Sprinkle with 1 teaspoon salt. Mash the garlic in the remaining ½ teaspoon salt and add with the cumin and pepper. Pour in the wine and bean stock (the liquid in which the beans were cooked). If there is not enough stock, add water to make 1½ cups. Cover the beans and bake at 300° for 6 hours. If the liquid boils away, add either more bean stock, water, or wine according to taste. Uncover during the last ½ hour of cooking. Makes 6 servings.

Lima Beans with Dill

You can dress up lima beans by tossing them with garlic-flavored butter and dill.

2 (10-oz.) pkg. frozen lima beans
1 onion
1 clove garlic
½ tsp. salt
2 tbsp. butter
Generous pinch of dill weed
½ tsp. lemon juice
Chopped parsley

Cook the lima beans according to package directions until tender but not mushy. Drain and set aside in a colander. Chop the onion and mash the garlic in the salt. Heat the butter in the pan in which the beans were cooked. Add the onion and garlic and cook until the onion is tender but not browned. Add the dill weed, which has been soaked in the lemon juice, and the cooked beans and toss to coat the beans thoroughly with the butter and seasonings. Taste and add more dill if you like. Heat to serving temperature and garnish with a sprinkling of chopped parsley. Makes 8 servings.

Toss-Fried Cauliflower, Chinese Style

Oyster sauce and a stir-fry method are all it takes to revolutionize cauliflower. In this type of cooking, all ingredients must be ready the moment the skillet is heated, for you will add them rapidly without time to chop or mix.

1 cauliflower
15 water chestnuts
3 green onions
1 tsp. cornstarch
1 tbsp. water
2 tbsp. soy sauce
1 tbsp. oyster sauce
1 tbsp. sake or other dry white wine
½ tsp. sugar
2 tbsp. vegetable or peanut oil
½ tsp. salt

Separate the cauliflower into flowerets and slice the flowerets to make thinner, fan-shaped pieces. Slice the water chestnuts in 2–3 pieces and chop the onions. Blend the cornstarch with the water and add the soy sauce, oyster sauce, sake, and sugar.

Parboil the flowerets in salted water 3 minutes and drain. Heat the oil in a skillet, add the flowerets and sprinkle with salt. Stir and cook for 1 minute. Stir in the water chestnuts and onions. Pour in the cornstarch mixture and toss and stir until the vegetables are coated with a glistening sauce. Makes 4 servings.

Chinese Vegetable Bake

A sort of casserole egg foo yung, this recipe came from Peking. It's a great company vegetable and an unusual main course for a luncheon.

3 eggs, separated
½ cup half-and-half
1 tsp. soy sauce
¼ tsp. salt
    Dash of garlic powder
¼ cup finely diced water chestnuts
1 cup coarsely chopped bean sprouts
1 green onion, chopped

FAR EAST SAUCE:

4 tsp. cornstarch
¼ cup soy sauce
¼ cup mirin or medium sweet sherry
1 cup water
1 small green onion, chopped

Beat the egg yolks until foamy. Add the half-and-half, soy sauce, salt, and garlic powder and beat again. Stir in the water chestnuts, bean sprouts, and green onion. Beat the egg whites until stiff and fold them into the vegetables. Pour into a buttered casserole and bake, uncovered, at 350° for 30 minutes.

To make the sauce, dissolve the cornstarch in the soy sauce and add the mirin and water. Bring to a boil and cook and stir until slightly thickened. Add the green onion just before serving. Pass the sauce separately with the casserole or pour a little over each serving. Makes 4 servings.

Braised Nappa Cabbage

The Chinese came to California to build railroads and incidentally added Cantonese cooking to our repertoire. From them we learned that the less you cook a vegetable, the better. One extra minute and this crispy dish will be limp and watery. Also called Chinese cabbage, nappa cabbage comes in bunches like celery but has wider, white stalks ending in frilly green tips. It bears no resemblance to ordinary head cabbage.

2 tbsp. bacon drippings
1 clove garlic
1 tsp. salt
6 cups coarsely chopped nappa cabbage (about a 1-lb. bunch)
Pinch of monosodium glutamate
Chopped green onions or chives

Heat the bacon drippings in a large saucepan. Mash the garlic in the salt and cook it a few seconds in the drippings. Raise the heat to high, add the cabbage and monosodium glutamate and toss with the drippings. Cover and cook 1½ minutes, no longer. Add no liquid, for the cabbage will produce its own. Garnish each serving with chopped green onions or chives. Makes 4 servings.

Peppers and Onions

This recipe drifted to Los Angeles from an Italian living in Phoenix, Arizona. It's as tasty as it is simple.

1 large red onion
1 green pepper
1 tbsp. olive oil
1 tbsp. butter
Salt

Slice the onion in rings and the pepper in strips. Heat the olive oil and butter in a skillet. Add the onion and green pepper and sprinkle with salt to taste. Cover and simmer until the vegetables are tender. Don't add any liquid because the vegetables will produce their own. If the onions are allowed to caramelize a little, the dish will taste even better. Makes 3 servings.

Seasoned Spinach

Creamed spinach is a standard dish, but you can improve it by adding onions and a bit of garlic.

2 (10-oz.) pkg. frozen chopped spinach
3 tbsp. butter
2 tbsp. flour
1 cup half-and-half
1 clove garlic
½ cup finely chopped onion
  Salt

Cook the spinach according to package directions and drain. Melt 2 tablespoons butter in a saucepan. Stir in the flour until smooth. Add the half-and-half and cook and stir until the white sauce thickens. Melt the remaining 1 tablespoon butter in a small skillet, add the garlic clove and onion and cook until the onion is wilted. Remove the garlic clove. Combine the spinach, onion and white sauce. Stir until well blended, season with salt to taste and heat to serving temperature. Makes 6 servings.

Sherried Rutabaga

Don't waste any loving care on the humble rutabaga. Just douse it with wine, shove it in the oven, and wait for its reappearance as a superior vegetable.

1 large rutabaga   *okay – takes much longer*
2 tbsp. butter   *than an hour to*
  Salt
  Pepper   *cook tender*
1 tsp. sugar
½ cup sherry

Peel the rutabaga and cut it in cubes. Dot the butter in a casserole, add the rutabaga, and sprinkle it with salt and pepper to taste and sugar. Add the sherry. Bake, covered, at 350° for 1 hour. Makes 4 servings.

Calabacitas con Rajas
(*Zucchini with Chile*)

Rajas are strips of chile that the Mexicans combine with cheese, meat, or in this case, with "calabacitas," which means little squash or zucchini.

3 large zucchini
1 large poblano chile or long green chile
1 small or medium onion
1 clove garlic
½ tsp. salt
3 tbsp. butter
2 tsp. chopped fresh basil
2 tbsp. cream

Cut each squash into 1½-inch sections and the sections into strips about ¼ inch thick. Blister the chile under the broiler, then peel it, remove the seeds, and cut it into thin strips about 1½ inches long. Cut the onion in thin slices and divide each slice into quarters. Mince the garlic and mash it in the salt.

Melt half the butter in a saucepan or skillet. Add the garlic and onion and cook until the onion is wilted. Add the zucchini sticks, the chile strips, the rest of the butter and the basil. Toss the vegetables lightly to mix. Add the cream, then cover and cook until the zucchini is tender, about 20–25 minutes. Makes 4 servings.

Stuffed Zucchini à la Española

This recipe for stuffed zucchini came from Spain a few decades after the hardy souls who settled California.

4 small zucchini
½ small onion
2 small tomatoes
½ clove garlic
Salt

1 tbsp. butter
Pepper
Pinch of oregano
¼ cup buttered bread crumbs
¼ cup freshly grated Parmesan cheese

Cook the zucchini about 10 minutes in boiling salted water. Do not overcook. Drain the zucchini, cut them in half lengthwise, and scoop out the pulp with a spoon. Be careful not to break the shells.

Mince the onion. Peel and chop the tomatoes. Crush the garlic in a little salt. Melt the butter in a skillet, add the onion and garlic, and cook until the onion is transparent. Add the tomatoes and simmer until most of the liquid from the tomatoes cooks away. Chop the zucchini pulp and add to the tomato mixture. Season with salt and pepper to taste and crumble in a little oregano.

Arrange the zucchini shells in a buttered baking dish and fill them with the vegetable mixture. Combine the bread crumbs and cheese and sprinkle a little over each zucchini half. Bake, uncovered, at 350° about 20 minutes. Makes 4 servings.

Spiced Banana Squash in Foil

Here is a vegetable that you can put in the oven and forget until dinner is served. Go as heavy on the sugar as you please—it only improves the flavor.

1 banana squash (about 1 lb.)
1½ tbsp. butter
Salt
⅓ cup brown sugar
Cinnamon
Ground ginger

Leave the squash in one piece and do not peel it. Set it on a large rectangle of aluminum foil, dot it with butter, and sprinkle with salt. Now sprinkle with the brown sugar and add a generous dash each of cinnamon and ginger, or as much as suits your taste. Wrap the foil over the squash and crimp it tightly to keep in the juices. Place in a baking pan and bake at 350° 1 hour or until the squash is tender. Makes 4 servings.

Curried Papaya Sambal

In India they curry everything, a custom I borrowed for this spicy-sweet meat accompaniment. Fresh papayas are in the markets most of the year here and make admirable curry material. Fresh pineapple is also available, but I prefer the canned for this recipe.

2 papayas
6 canned pineapple rings
6 tbsp. butter
¼ cup brown sugar
¼ cup sherry
1 tsp. curry
¼ tsp. salt
  Bottled chutney

Cut the papayas in half, scoop out the seeds and cut the halves into strips. Peel the strips and cut them into chunks. Divide the pineapple rings into small chunks. Melt the butter in a large skillet and stir in the sugar, sherry, curry, and salt. Simmer until the sugar is melted and the mixture is hot. Add the papaya and pineapple, stirring gently so as not to crush the papaya. Leave the fruit in the sauce only until warmed, then serve immediately. Place a dab of chutney on each serving. Makes 4–6 servings.

Garlic Tostones

The big bland cooking bananas called plantains are fundamental to Caribbean and Latin American cooking. If you can get them, try this crusty substitute for potatoes.

2 medium plantains
2 tbsp. butter
2 tbsp. oil
1 clove garlic, crushed
  Garlic salt

Peel the plantains, cut them crosswise in ½-inch slices and drop the slices into salted water. Heat 1 tablespoon butter and 1 tablespoon oil with the garlic clove in a large skillet. Drain the plantain slices and cook them on each side until tender. Remove the cooked slices from the skillet and set them on paper towels to drain. One by one, place the slices between sheets of wax paper and press them with a mallet, the bottom of a jar or other flat object until they flatten out and are about ¼ inch thick. Add the remaining oil and butter to the skillet and cook the flattened slices on each side until crusty. Do not crowd the pan. Add more oil and butter if necessary. Drain the tostones on paper towels and sprinkle with garlic salt. Makes 4–5 servings.

Chip Potatoes

You'll forget French fries when you've tasted potatoes cooked this way. They're marvelous with roasts and irresistible to men.

6 medium potatoes
¼ cup oil
  Salt

Peel the potatoes and cut each lengthwise into three sections. Cut each section lengthwise into three more sections, making slices about the length and width of a finger.

Pour the oil into a large baking pan, add the potatoes and shake the pan to coat them with oil. Bake, uncovered, at 400° until the potatoes start to brown. Turn them over, lower the heat to 350° and bake until the potatoes are well browned, about 1 hour altogether. Drain off excess oil, sprinkle the potatoes with salt and serve. Makes 4 servings.

Papas con Chile
(*Potatoes with Chiles*)

So many kinds of chiles are marketed in California that they wind up in everything except dessert. Here they enliven a savory potato casserole.

4 medium boiling potatoes
3 long green chiles (mild)
1 large onion
2½ tbsp. butter
1 tbsp. flour
1 cup milk
½ cup chicken stock
1 tsp. salt
⅓ cup chopped toasted almonds
½ tsp. basil
¼ tsp. freshly ground black pepper

Peel the potatoes, slice them paper thin (I use the cutting blade on a vegetable grater for this) and place them in cold water to cover. Place the chiles under the broiler until their skins darken and pop, then peel them and chop coarsely. Slice the onion and separate it into rings.

Melt 1½ tablespoons butter in a saucepan. Blend in the flour until smooth. Add the milk and cook, stirring constantly, until thickened. Add the chicken stock and salt.

Dot the bottom of a 2½ or 3-quart casserole with the remaining 1 tablespoon butter. Add one-third of the drained potatoes. Top with one-third each of the onion rings, chiles, and almonds. Sprinkle with a pinch of the basil. Make two more layers in this fashion. Then pour the white sauce over and sprinkle with the pepper. Cover the casserole and bake ½ hour at 350°. Uncover and bake 45 minutes longer, or until the potatoes are tender. Makes 6 servings.

Potatoes and Onions

This variation on the preceding potato casserole eliminates the chiles and gains new flavor from garlic.

5 small boiling potatoes
1 small onion
1 clove garlic
½ tsp. salt
2 tbsp. butter
  Pepper
  Fresh or dried thyme
1 cup milk
  Chopped parsley

Peel the potatoes and slice them paper thin, placing the slices in cold water to prevent discoloration. Cut the onion in thin slices and separate the slices into rings. Mash the garlic in the salt. Melt 1 tablespoon butter in a skillet, add the onion and garlic and cook until the onion is soft.

Drain the potatoes and place a layer of the slices in a buttered casserole. Top the potatoes with some of the garlic-flavored onion rings. Dot with some of the remaining butter, sprinkle with a little pepper and a pinch of thyme. Make layers in this fashion until the ingredients are used up. Then pour in the milk. Cover and bake at 350° for ½ hour. Uncover and bake ½ hour to 45 minutes longer, or until the potatoes are tender. Garnish each serving with chopped parsley. Makes 4–5 servings.

Garlic Mashed Potatoes

You can't improve well-made mashed potatoes unless you add a little garlic.

3 large boiling potatoes
2 large cloves garlic
1¼ tsp. salt
1½ tbsp. butter
¼ cup milk

Peel the potatoes and cut them in quarters. Place them in a large saucepan and cover with cold water. Peel the garlic cloves, cut them in 3 or 4 pieces and add to the potatoes. Add 1 teaspoon salt and put the potatoes on to boil. Cover and cook until the potatoes can be pierced easily with a fork. Drain the potatoes and remove the garlic. Now add the remaining ¼ teaspoon salt and mash the potatoes, keeping the pan over very low heat. Add the butter and beat. Add the milk gradually and beat until the potatoes are soft and fluffy. You may need more or less milk depending upon the consistency of the potatoes. Makes 4 servings.

RICE

I am a rice experimentalist. I like to work with different types— long-grain rice shipped from Jojutla and Guadalajara in Mexico; the extraordinary basmati rice of India; the sticky, glutinous rice used to make certain Oriental desserts; the short-grain, blue rose and pearl rices, which produce fluffy bowlfuls to accompany sukiyaki; and when I'm in a hurry, the faithful, all-American instant rice.

I can't resist a new variety. Not long ago, in Los Angeles' Little Tokyo, I discovered Kokuho rice. A huge black and chartreuse sign advertised its arrival, and the shopkeeper described it as a blend of glutinous and California rice. It was by far the best, she said, and correspondingly more expensive. I went out with five pounds.

It may surprise some to learn that California is an important rice-producing state. All of our rice is either medium or short grain. The medium grain is most commonly used, and much of the short grain is exported.

Of the many methods of rice cookery, I find the Mexican and Far Eastern techniques both easy and consistently successful. The Mexican method is explained in chapter 7, but can be applied to other types of recipes.

The Far Eastern technique is best for steamed rice to accompany an Oriental dinner. This method starts with soaking the rice in cool water for an hour or more and then washing it until the water remains fairly clear. Instead of frying the rice, as in the Mexican method, you put it on to boil in water to cover generously. After it has boiled up well, you steam it gently, covered, over low heat for about 10 minutes. When the rice has absorbed almost all the water, you remove the cover and turn the heat up high to steam out the last bit of liquid. Then you cover the rice and let it sit for another 10 minutes before serving.

One secret of rice cookery—most recipes tell you to use twice as much water as rice, for example, 2 cups water to 1 cup rice. But ignore this and use a little less, say 1¾ cups water to 1 cup rice, and you will find it easier to avoid mush and produce flaky, tender, dry rice.

Allow for tomatoes and other soupy ingredients when judging the amount of liquid you will need. And don't be afraid you are using too little. I once cooked a short-grain rice following the Far Eastern method and using equal parts rice and water. The results surprised me too. The rice was perfect.

White Rice with Onions

This simply seasoned rice goes with almost anything.

> 1 cup long-grain rice
> 1 small onion
> 1 clove garlic
> 1 tsp. salt
> 2 tbsp. lard
> 1¾ cups water
> 1 tbsp. butter
> Finely chopped green onion tops

Soak the rice in hot water for 15 minutes. Drain and wash until the water runs clear. Spread the rice out on a platter to dry. Chop the onion and mash the garlic in ½ teaspoon salt. Melt the lard in a skillet or heavy saucepan. Add the onion, garlic and rice and cook until the rice turns faintly golden. Add the water and remaining ½ teaspoon salt. Bring to a boil, cover, and let boil gently until the rice absorbs most of the water. Then simmer over low heat (I usually place the pan on an asbestos mat) until the rest of the water is absorbed and the grains are separate. Dot the butter over the rice, toss gently with a fork, and serve sprinkled with green onion tops. Makes 4 servings.

Curried Rice

In Southeast Asia, they cook rice with coconut milk, an idea that adds an exotic note to this recipe. I use canned coconut milk, but if you can't get it, you can scald milk, or a combination of half milk and half water, with a little shredded coconut, let it steep, and then squeeze the liquid out of the coconut.

        1 cup rice
        1 clove garlic
        1 tsp. salt
        1 onion
    1½ tbsp. butter
        1 tsp. curry powder
    1¼ cups water
        ½ cup coconut milk
        ¼ tsp. freshly ground black pepper

Soak the rice in hot water for 15 minutes. Wash it thoroughly in several waters, then drain it, and spread it out on a platter to dry. Mash the garlic in ½ teaspoon salt and chop the onion. Melt the butter in a large skillet, add the onion and garlic, and cook until the onion is tender. Add the curry powder and rice and cook for about 5 minutes. Add the water and coconut milk. Season with the pepper and remaining ½ teaspoon salt. Cover and let boil gently until most of the liquid is absorbed, then simmer over low heat until the rice is dry and flaky. Fluff with a fork. Makes 4 servings.

Indonesian Coconut Rice

Talk of Jogjakarta and the great shrine of Borobudur punctuate conversation when Ann Soeleiman hosts a dinner. Ann cooks coconut rice with the know-how of the native Indonesian. Here is my imitation.

　1　cup long-grain rice
　1　(8-oz.) can coconut milk
　¾　cup water
　1　tsp. chicken-seasoned stock base
　2　tbsp. shredded coconut
　½　bay leaf
　½　tsp. salt
　　　Onion Crisps (optional)

Soak the rice in hot water for 15 minutes. Drain, then wash in cold water until the water runs clear. Drain the rice. Combine the coconut milk with water, chicken-seasoned stock base, shredded coconut and the bay leaf. Bring to a boil. Remove the bay leaf, stir in the rice and add the salt. Cover and boil gently until the rice has absorbed most of the liquid. Then simmer over low heat until the rice is dry and flaky. Serve with onion crisps sprinkled over the top. Makes 4 servings.

ONION CRISPS
　Onions
　Oil for deep frying
　Salt
　Sugar

Slice as many onions as you like paper-thin, then cut each slice into halves or quarters depending upon the size of the onion. Drop a few pieces of onion at a time into very hot oil. When the onions have shriveled up and turned golden, lift them out and drain them on paper toweling. When all the onions are fried, sprinkle them with salt and a bit of sugar. Serve them as a garnish for rice, string beans or other vegetables.

Chinese Fried Rice

A Chinese chef reigned briefly at the house where I lived at Stanford University. His fried rice was so good that I ate to the point of illness. And when Wong quit one day, a hapless throng followed him out the door and up the street. I have never tasted the likes of Wong's rice again, but this recipe is also one of my favorites.

    2 dried black Oriental mushrooms
    1 clove garlic
    3 green onions
    2 tbsp. oil
 3½ cups cooked long-grain rice
       Dash of salt
    ½ cup finely diced cooked chicken or pork
    3 tbsp. soy sauce
    1 egg

Soak the mushrooms in hot water until they swell up and soften. Chop them very fine. Mince the garlic and chop the onions. Heat the oil in a skillet, add the garlic and cook until it begins to brown. Add the rice and stir to break up any lumps. Sprinkle with a little salt. Add the meat, mushrooms and onions and mix well. Add the soy sauce and stir until well blended. Beat the egg until foamy. Make sure the rice is very hot and stir in the egg just before serving. Makes 5–6 servings.

Spiced Rice

The devotees of a Hindu swami in Los Angeles introduced me to basmati rice, which comes from India. They use it for their religious feasts and value it for its special flavor. I found some in a tiny Middle Eastern store where the customers spoke no English. It is the most elegant rice I have encountered—silky and firm, yet tender when cooked, and exceptionally long grained. It is also quite expensive, but well worth the price. This regal rice should be treated simply, as in the following recipe that gives it a delicate perfume and golden color.

1 cup basmati rice or other long-grain rice
2 tbsp. pressed coconut oil or other bland oil
1¾ cup water
⅛ tsp. turmeric
⅛ tsp. cumin
⅛ tsp. cardamom
1 tsp. salt

Soak the rice in hot water for 15 minutes. Drain and rinse in cold water until the water runs clear. Spread out to dry on a platter. Heat the coconut oil in a heavy skillet. Fry the rice until lightly golden. Add the water, turmeric, cumin, cardamom, and salt. Stir to distribute the spices. Cover and let boil until most of the water is absorbed. Then place on an asbestos mat over low heat for 20–25 minutes, or until the water is absorbed and the rice is flaky. Makes 4 servings.

Sushi Rice

The Japanese flavor rice with sugar, vinegar, and salt and form it into little patties that they top with raw fish. This is called sushi. If you eliminate the raw fish, which has little appeal for the average American, you are left with an interesting accompaniment for cooked fish. I garnish the little mounds with a sprinkling of powdered seaweed (aonoriko), which I buy in shaker bottles in Japanese stores. But you can substitute chopped parsley, chives, or any herb you like with rice. However, you must use a short-grain rice, which will give a slightly sticky texture. Long-grain rice will not work in this recipe.

1 cup short-grain rice
1 cup water
1 tsp. instant minced onion
1 tsp. salt
  Dash of monosodium glutamate
5 tsp. vinegar
2 tsp. sugar
  Aonoriko (powdered seaweed)

Soak the rice in cold water for 1–2 hours. Squeeze the rice, scrubbing it a little with your hands. Pour off the water, which will now be cloudy. Add new water and wash the rice again. Continue until the water is almost clear. Drain the rice and place in a heavy saucepan with 1 cup water, the minced onion, salt, and monosodium glutamate. Cover and bring to a boil. Turn the heat very low and let the rice sit 15 minutes. Uncover and turn the heat to high for 30 seconds to 1 minute. Cover the rice, remove from heat and let stand 15 minutes. Heat the vinegar and sugar until the sugar dissolves. Work the vinegar and sugar through the rice with a fork. Pack the rice into small custard cups to mold it, then turn out to serve. Sprinkle aonoriko over each serving. Makes 6 servings.

Quick Vermouth Pilaf

Wine with rice? Why not, when the two blend into a dish that combines epicurean interest with speed?

⅓ cup dry vermouth
⅓ cup beef stock
⅓ cup water
1 tbsp. butter
1 tsp. instant minced onion
¼ tsp. sage
½ tsp. salt
¼ tsp. freshly ground black pepper
  Dash of garlic powder
1⅓ cups instant rice
  Chopped parsley

Combine vermouth, beef stock, water, butter, minced onion, sage, salt, pepper, and garlic powder in a saucepan. Bring to a boil. Add the rice and stir. Cover and place on an asbestos mat over low heat for 5 minutes. Fluff up with a fork and serve sprinkled with chopped parsley. Makes 3–4 servings.

5

The Main Course

The main course for dinner in California is anything but predictable. While the Chinese in San Francisco are barbecuing pork, the Yugoslav fishermen of San Pedro are putting their catch into a hearty stew called cioppino. In San Diego, the Portuguese are at work on tripe or cod. And Mexicans everywhere are experiencing what John Steinbeck described in *Tortilla Flat* as "a golden warmth glowing like a hot enchilada in one's stomach."

One would expect such colorful and varied eating patterns in a part of the world that has attracted many ethnic groups. But has this savory melting pot tipped its wealth into the population at large?

To find the answer, I turned to what I consider the ultimate expression of conventional Americana, a church potluck dinner. The church I chose is a large one on a fashionable street in the heart of Los Angeles and caters to no particular nationality group.

Its dinners are, apparently, famous. A long line of people waited to buy tickets, the huge dining room was packed, and a separate room had to be set aside for desserts. In the main room, the buffet tables would have stretched half a block if someone had put them together. They were crammed with a feast produced in the kitchens of the members. Potato salad, baked beans, tuna casserole, and brownies? Not on your life. There were Swiss beans, eggplant Parmigiana, vitello tonnato, Mandarin beef, Turkish meat balls, a Japanese pork dish called buta tofu, stir-fried chicken, soy baked chicken, taco chicken and chicken mole.

I was particularly taken with the mole, an oldtime Mexican dish featuring a sauce of chiles, nuts, and chocolate. This up-to-date American version was made with a Hershey bar.

If I had to select any particular food as typical of California, it would, I suppose, be barbecued beef. Beef is our number-one agricultural crop, if you can call cattle a crop. And cattle accompanied the first Spaniards who ventured here in 1769. In the days of the haciendas and vaqueros, great hunks of freshly slaughtered beef were seared over the fire and served with frijoles, a chile salsa and tortillas, which were used instead of forks to scoop up the food. We still have old-fashioned barbecues of this sort, only the beef is not quite so fresh from the hoof. For the most part, our home-barbecued beef takes the form of steaks from the supermarket.

Barbecuing, which derives its name from the Spanish word, "barbacoa," is an old art in California. But centuries of practice do not make perfect, and some of our chefs do more charring than searing—thus the smoke signals that each summer announce the start of what we call the "barbecue season."

Actually, we cook outdoors all year, and every home has some sort of barbecue facility, ranging from expensive appliances with artificial coals to the tiny hibachis that apartment dwellers set outside their doors. There are even tinier hibachis for barbecuing cocktail appetizers indoors.

You will not learn the rules of outdoor cookery in this chapter, for I am not one of those who have mastered the element of fire, or rather those elaborate arrangements of coals and peculiar methods of ignition that capture it in the barbecue. To be honest, I would rather leave such messy chores to men. It gives them a chance to wear the billowing chefs hats and slogan-covered aprons that people delight in giving them on Father's Day.

Atmosphere is a superb seasoner and perhaps that is one secret of the barbecue. I remember a hot, clear night in the San Joaquin Valley. There were several of us; we were on a ranch and had taken a late horseback ride. One of the group, an Armenian, had arranged to surprise us with a midnight snack of barbecued shish kebab. The moon streamed down, the sycamores rustled, and the only other sounds were the shuffling of the horses and the sizzling of the spicy meat juices as they dripped onto the coals. You can't find that sort of flavor in a restaurant.

Often fondness for a certain food stems from its connection with such an experience. One of my favorite meals was based on nothing more than hot tortillas purchased from a place in Puerto Vallarta, Mexico, called (in Spanish) The Hygienic Tortilla Factory. The tortillas were supplemented by a beer from a stand at the beach. And the blue sky and bluer sea turned this simple repast into a feast that I would not have traded at that moment for the best in Paris.

You can get awfully good tortillas in Los Angeles, too, at little more than a dime a dozen. I smear them with butter, heat them until the butter bubbles and sprinkle them with salt. With a salad, that makes a rudimentary, but very pleasing, main course for lunch-in-a-hurry.

Occasionally, one hungers over descriptions of exotic delicacies as served far away in their native lands. The truth is, the fields are sometimes greener and the food better at home. I had a terrible paella in Madrid and a superb one at a ranch just outside Los Angeles. The cook, a dancer, was pure Spanish. I liked the sukiyaki in Japan, but found it extraordinary in a humble home in East Los Angeles. The chef in this case was a Japanese who cooked as therapy for homesickness.

If I have any philosophy about the main course, it is variety. Extravagant meals night after night would become a bore. Even the meat, vegetable, and potato routine needs breaking up. I have tried the chrysanthemum pot of the Chinese, the falafil of the Egyptians and the bulky nacatamales of the Nicaraguans. But change does not have to be dramatic. Like almost everyone, I grew up with spaghetti. Now I serve linguini. This simple switch from round to flat pasta makes a surprising difference, for texture is a more important element in taste than you might believe.

Change need not be expensive either. The simple luxury of homemade buns turns hamburgers into a delicacy beyond the reach of lonely restaurant diners, padded though their expense accounts may be.

I like to experiment with unfamiliar foods. My current project is salt cod, which is foreign to my kitchen although not to my palate. I boldly bought a chunk in a Latin market and stored it in the freezer while I weighed the lures of mouth-watering recipes from Spain, Portugal, and Mexico. But I admit the pull of the old ways is strong. Fascinating as its possibilities may be, the salt cod is still in the freezer.

Chicken Ajo

Ajo is the Spanish word for garlic, and we produce enough of it in California to decimate, with a breath of wind, most of the world's garlic haters. I can't imagine there being many, though, because to me garlic is superb and a basic seasoning. Don't be afraid of the amount in the following recipe. The flavor mellows considerably in the cooking, and you won't need to spend the rest of the evening alone.

 4 chicken legs and thighs, or other chicken pieces
 3 cloves garlic
 1 tsp. salt
 2 tsp. fresh oregano (½ tsp. dried)
 1 tbsp. oil
 ¼ cup brandy
 ½ medium onion, chopped
 3 whole sprigs fresh oregano, if available
 3 tbsp. butter
 ¼ cup white wine
 2 tsp. flour
 1 cup chicken stock
 2 tbsp. cream

Separate the chicken legs from the thighs, making 8 pieces. In a mortar, mash and blend the garlic cloves, salt, and the 2 teaspoons oregano. Stir in the oil. Place the chicken pieces in a bowl or casserole and rub them thoroughly with this mixture. Add the brandy and onion and place the whole sprigs of oregano on top. Cover, refrigerate, and marinate overnight, or preferably for two days, turning the chicken pieces occasionally.

Melt the butter in a skillet, add the drained chicken pieces, and brown well on each side. Add the wine, the onions from the marinade, and a little of the liquid. Cover the chicken and simmer until tender, about 1 hour, adding the rest of the marinade during the cooking.

When the chicken is done, remove it to a serving platter and keep hot. Blend the flour with the pan juices and stir until smooth. Add the chicken stock and bring slowly to a boil, scraping up the pan. When the gravy thickens slightly, stir in the cream. Pour the gravy into a sauceboat and pass it with the chicken. Makes 4 servings.

Chicken Sebastopol

California-made cider, apple brandy, and wine blend in the sauce for a particularly elegant chicken dish.

    4　chicken breasts
   ⅓　cup flour
   ½　tsp. salt
   ¼　tsp. pepper
   ¼　cup butter
   1　jigger apple brandy
   ¾　cup apple cider
   ½　cup dry white wine
   1　medium onion
½–1　tsp. sage
     Salt
   ½　lb. mushrooms
   ½　cup half-and-half

Shake the chicken breasts one at a time in a paper bag with the flour, salt, and pepper. Heat the butter in a large skillet, add the chicken breasts, and brown them. When the chicken is browned on both sides, pour the apple brandy over it, and ignite (use a long-stemmed match). When the flame dies away, add the cider and wine. Chop the onion and add it to the skillet. Sprinkle with sage and salt to taste. Cover and simmer until the chicken is tender, about 1 hour. Slice the mushrooms and add them during the last 15 minutes of cooking time. Remove the chicken to a platter and keep warm. Add the half-and-half to the skillet and simmer over low heat, stirring and scraping up the pan, until the sauce is thickened. Strain, if desired, and serve in a sauceboat with the chicken. Makes 4 servings.

Japanese Chicken in Foil

Sansho is a Japanese pepper with a unique fragrance. Combined with lemon and fresh ginger, it adds subtle, interesting flavor to this chicken dish. If you don't have sansho, use regular pepper. You will still enjoy an important advantage of this recipe, which is convenience. Ideal for company, the foil-wrapped packets of chicken go into the oven an hour and a half before dinner. To serve, you simply place a packet on each guest's plate.

For each serving you will need:

1 medium chicken breast
2 tsp. butter
Salt
Sansho or other pepper
2 thin slices lemon
3 large mushrooms, sliced
¼ tsp. grated ginger root
¼ tsp. sugar
1 tsp. soy sauce
1 tsp. sake or other dry white wine

Very good

Bone each chicken breast. Place a little butter in the center of a 12-inch length of aluminum foil and lay the chicken breast on it, skin side down. Sprinkle generously with salt and sansho. Lay on the lemon slices, then the mushrooms. Sprinkle again with salt and sansho. Dot with the remaining butter and sprinkle with ginger and sugar. Bring two opposite edges of foil together over the chicken and fold over to form a tightly closed seam. Fold one open end in toward the center of the packet, crimping tightly. Leave the other end open. When all the packets are prepared, hold each on end and pour in the soy sauce and sake. Now close the packets securely. Place them in a baking pan and bake at 350° 1½ hours.

Chicken Makahiki

I was vacationing a few hours west and south of California— in Honolulu, to be exact. The palm trees were waving, the blue sea rolled in and out, and I was eating a marvelous dish of chicken prepared with coconut milk and bean sprouts. The scene was an outdoor dining area at the Hilton Hawaiian Village Hotel. Here is my mainland re-creation of the chicken. For maximum flavor, prepare it well in advance of serving.

    3 large chicken breasts
    1 small onion
    1 tsp. salt
    ¼ cup butter
    ⅓ cup flour
    1 cup half-and-half
    1 cup chicken broth
    1 (8-oz.) can coconut milk
    ½ cup shredded fresh coconut or ¼ cup packaged
        shredded coconut
    2 cups bean sprouts

Place the chicken breasts in a large saucepan and add water almost to the top of the chicken. Add the onion, coarsely chopped, and ½ teaspoon salt. Cover and simmer until the chicken is tender, 1–1½ hours. Remove the chicken (save the broth) and bone it. Coarsely shred the meat and place it in a 2-quart casserole.

Melt the butter in a saucepan and stir in the flour until smooth. Gradually add the half-and-half, stirring until smooth. Now add the broth from cooking the chicken, coconut milk, shredded coconut, and ½ teaspoon salt. Bring to a boil over moderate heat, stirring constantly. When the sauce is thick, pour it over the chicken. Cool and refrigerate the casserole. When reheating, stir in the bean sprouts and bake, uncovered, at 325° for 1 hour, or until hot and bubbly. Makes 6 servings.

Five Fragrance Chicken

Chinese five spice powder is an excellent seasoning for chicken and barbecued meats and superb on, of all things, apple pie. The ketjap in this recipe is a sweetened soy sauce used in Indonesian cooking. You can substitute regular soy sauce and a dash of sugar or regular soy sauce and a sweet sherry.

3 chicken breasts
1 clove garlic
2 tbsp. oil
½ tsp. Chinese five spice powder
¼ cup dry sherry
2 tsp. fresh lime juice
2 tbsp. ketjap
½ tsp. salt
Dash of pepper
1 tsp. cornstarch
2 tsp. water

Bone and skin the chicken breasts and cut them into bite-size chunks. Mince the garlic clove. Heat the oil in a large skillet, add the garlic and sauté a few moments. Add the chicken and cook until lightly browned. Sprinkle with the five spice powder and add the sherry, lime juice, ketjap, salt, and pepper. Cover and simmer 4 to 6 minutes, until the chicken is thoroughly cooked. Blend the cornstarch and water, add to the skillet and stir until the sauce thickens and coats each piece of chicken. Makes 4 servings.

Creamed Chicken with Jicama

This recipe is really glorified creamed chicken with jicama added for fun. I have heard that Orientals use the crisp, white-fleshed jicama when they can't get water chestnuts. But this doesn't seem likely because water chestnuts are easy to find, while jicama is comparatively rare. If you can't get either, put in something else like, maybe, dumplings.

    4 medium chicken breasts
    ⅓ cup flour
    ½ tsp. salt
    ¼ tsp. pepper
    ¼ cup butter
    1 medium onion
    ½ cup vermouth
    ¼ cup water
    ¼ lb. mushrooms
    ½ cup half-and-half
    2 tsp. soy sauce
    ½ cup diced jicama

Shake the chicken breasts one at a time in a paper bag with the flour, salt, and pepper. Heat the butter in a large skillet, add the chicken breasts and brown them. Coarsely chop the onion and cook it with the chicken. When the chicken is browned, add the vermouth and water. Cover and simmer gently until the chicken is tender, about 1 hour. Add more vermouth or water if the liquid boils away. Slice the mushrooms and add them during the last 20 minutes of cooking time. When the chicken is done, remove it to a serving platter, and keep it warm in the oven. Leave the mushrooms in the skillet and add the half-and-half, soy sauce, and jicama. Stir and scrape up the pan. Cook the sauce until it thickens, then pour it over the chicken breasts. Makes 4 servings.

Paella Frontera

I bought my paella pan in Tijuana, which inspired both the name ("frontera" means border) and some of the ingredients of this paella. Even the saffron I use is Mexican. It comes from a different plant than Spanish saffron, is much cheaper, and so I use it generously.

This recipe eliminates the multitudes of seafood which deter many would-be paella makers and concentrates on chicken and chorizo, which are easier to obtain. Except for the preliminary simmering of the chorizos, all of the cooking is done in the one pan. I think that recipes requiring you to use three or four other utensils before combining the ingredients in the paella pan are wasteful and silly.

  1½ cups short-grain rice
   2 Spanish chorizos
 1–2 long green chiles
   1 chicken plus 1 leg and thigh
   3 tbsp. butter
   1 tbsp. olive oil
  ¼ tsp. mild chili powder
   1 medium onion
   1 clove garlic
   1 tsp. salt
   1 cup chicken stock
   1 cup canned tomatoes with their liquid
   1 bay leaf
  ¼ tsp. cumin
  ¼ tsp. pepper
  ½ tsp. Mexican saffron sprigs
   1 cup hot water
   1 cup frozen peas
     Lemon wedges, strips of pimiento or tomato wedges, cilantro sprigs or parsley for garnish

Soak the rice (I use the blue rose variety) in hot water for 1 hour. Rub with the hands and drain. Wash the rice until the water runs fairly clear, then drain it, and spread it out on a platter.

Place the chorizos in a small skillet and add a little water, but not enough to cover them. Cover the pan and simmer the chorizos for 30 minutes, being careful not to let them dry out and burn. Drain. When cool, slice the chorizos diagonally in ¼-inch slices.

Place the chiles under the broiler until the skins blister and pop, then peel, seed and chop them.

Cut the chicken in serving pieces, separating the thighs from the legs. Bone the breast and cut it in quarters. Reserve the back and neck for making stock.

Heat the butter and oil in a paella pan, large skillet or heavy, shallow casserole. Add the chicken pieces and brown them on both sides. Sprinkle them with the chili powder as they cook. Add the onion, chopped, and the garlic, mashed in ½ teaspoon salt. Cook until the onion is tender. Add the chicken stock, tomatoes, chiles, bay leaf, cumin, the remaining ½ teaspoon salt, and the pepper. Cover the pan. (I use aluminum foil plus my largest lid, which is not big enough to cover my paella pan by itself.) Simmer 30 minutes.

Now crush the saffron in 1 tablespoon of the hot water. Add the remaining water to the saffron and pour it into the skillet. Sprinkle the rice evenly around the pan and push it down under the liquid. Cover and simmer 20 minutes. Now sprinkle the peas over the rice, but do not mix. Arrange the chorizo slices in an attractive pattern on top of the paella. Cover and simmer gently until the peas are tender and most of the liquid is absorbed, about 15 minutes. Keep the heat low enough so the rice doesn't stick to the pan. Uncover, garnish with lemon wedges, pimiento, and cilantro and serve from the pan at the table. Makes 4 servings.

Beef and Water Chestnuts

Chinese cooking is simple, rapid, and tasty. This dish combines Chinese methods and ingredients with a French touch, the de-glazing of the pan with wine. The meat and water chestnuts will appear silky and glistening with sauce, but there should be no runny excess of liquid.

1½ lbs. flank steak
6 tbsp. soy sauce
¼ tsp. salt
3 tsp. cornstarch
½ tsp. sugar
1 (8½-oz.) can water chestnuts
1 tbsp. oil
6 tbsp. white wine
¼ cup water
2 tbsp. oyster sauce

Have the butcher put the steak through the tenderizer. Cut the steak into strips about 2 inches long, ½-inch wide and ¼-inch thick. Place the strips in a bowl and add 4 tablespoons of the soy sauce, the salt, 1 teaspoon cornstarch, and the sugar. Work the seasonings thoroughly into the meat and let marinate for at least ½ hour. Drain the water chestnuts and cut each into 3–4 slices.

Heat the oil in a heavy skillet over high heat. Add the steak strips and toss and cook them rapidly until browned. Remove the meat to a platter, lower the heat and deglaze the pan with the wine. Add the water chestnuts and simmer them briefly. Dissolve the remaining 2 teaspoons cornstarch in the water and add the oyster sauce and 2 tablespoons soy sauce. Pour this mixture into the skillet, add the beef, and toss and cook until the sauce thickens and coats the beef and water chestnuts. Makes 4 servings.

Danish Steak with Onions

Caramelized onions make a wonderful topping for steak, whether it's served in Copenhagen or in Solvang, the Danish community in southern California.

2 large onions
2 tbsp. butter
¼ tsp. salt
4½ tsp. sugar
4 steaks
2 tbsp. dry white wine

Cut the onions in thin slices. Heat the butter in a skillet, add the onions and sprinkle them with salt. Cover and simmer until the onions are tender. Uncover, sprinkle with sugar and cook over high heat, stirring constantly, until the onions are lightly browned.

Meanwhile, broil the steaks to the desired degree of doneness. Drain off excess drippings. Pour in the wine and scrape up the pan, letting the wine boil until it is reduced by half. Pour the wine into the skillet with the onions and stir. Serve each steak topped with onions. Makes 4 servings.

Steaks with Sherry-Oyster Sauce

I borrowed from the Chinese for this simple sauce that enhances a good steak without masking the flavor.

2–3 green onions
½ clove garlic
4 steaks
⅓ cup dry sherry
4 tsp. oyster sauce
4 tsp. soy sauce
2 tbsp. brandy
1 tbsp. butter

Chop the onions and mince the garlic. Broil the steaks to the desired degree of doneness. Remove the steaks from the skillet and deglaze the pan with the sherry. Add the onions, garlic, oyster sauce, soy sauce, brandy, and butter. Simmer briefly to blend and pour a little of the sauce over each steak. Makes 4 servings.

Steaks with Wine and Chile

Another approach to steaks calls for red wine, chile, and the coffee left over from breakfast.

1 clove garlic
2 green onions
4–6 steaks
2 tbsp. cold strong coffee
3 tbsp. butter
1–2 tbsp. chopped long green chile
½ cup red wine
Salt
Pepper

Mince the garlic and chop the onions. Broil the steaks to the desired degree of doneness, remove to a heated platter and keep warm. Deglaze the pan with the coffee. Add the butter, garlic, onions, chile, and wine. Season with salt and pepper to taste. Reduce the sauce until thick and pour over each serving of steak. Makes 4–6 servings.

Ginger Beef Frank Wong

Frank Wong was born in Kwangtung province and studied cooking in Hong Kong. When he came to my house to prepare a Chinese dinner, he reviewed the ingredients I had organized, politely set them aside and made this version of the main dish.

1½ lbs. flank steak

THE MARINADE:

¼ cup soy sauce
½ tsp. sesame oil
1½ tsp. sugar
1½ tsp. cornstarch
¼ tsp. salt
Dash of pepper

3 green onions
3 tbsp. shredded ginger root

THE SAUCE:

1 tsp. cornstarch
1 tbsp. water
2 tbsp. soy sauce
1 tbsp. oyster sauce
2 tbsp. peanut oil

Have the butcher put the steak through the tenderizer once. Slice the steak across the grain into sections about 1½ inches wide. Now slice each section crosswise (with the grain) into strips about ¼ inch wide. Place the strips in a bowl and add the soy sauce, sesame oil, sugar, cornstarch, salt, and pepper. Work this marinade thoroughly into the meat with chopsticks.

Slice the green onions into 1-inch lengths, then shred each section lengthwise. To shred the ginger root, take a chunk of root, peel it, cut it into thin slices, and shred. Combine the sauce ingredients—cornstarch, water, soy sauce, and oyster sauce—in a small bowl.

Heat the oil in a large, heavy skillet over high heat. Add the ginger root and onions. Toss and stir constantly for a few seconds. Now add the meat, keeping the heat high. Toss and cook until brown. This should be done as quickly as possible. Now add the sauce ingredients, stirring to coat the meat evenly. Stir and cook until each piece of meat is coated and glistening and the sauce is slightly thickened. There should be no pool of excess sauce. Serve immediately. Makes 6 servings.

Beef and Tofu

Very good — serve with rice

Tofu, or soy bean curd, is a great meat stretcher, and you will find budget-minded Oriental dishes that are heavy on the tofu and include only a few strips of meat. This dish works the other way around, but you could increase the amount of curd and decrease the beef if you prefer. I buy tofu in Japanese markets. It is formed in ¾-pound blocks and packed with liquid in a plastic container. You slice off what you need and cut it into cubes, bars or smaller blocks as desired.

1 lb. top round or sirloin
1 medium onion
4 green onions
2 tbsp. suet or butter
6 tbsp. soy sauce
3 tbsp. sake
3 tbsp. sugar
1 cup or more cubed soy bean curd

Included sautéed mushrooms ... other veg. Cook beef first rapidly and remove, will toughen otherwise

Cut the beef into thin strips. Slice the onion in thin slices. Cut the green onions into 1-inch sections and sliver the sections lengthwise.

Heat the suet or butter in a heavy skillet, add the meat, and cook and stir it until browned. Add the onions and cook them as the meat browns. Combine the soy sauce, sake, and sugar and pour over the meat and onions. Simmer 1–2 minutes until the meat is cooked. Add the bean curd to the skillet and simmer only long enough to heat it through. Makes 4 servings.

Quick Chuck

Every cook needs the sort of quick dish that cooks unattended and comes out tasting terrific. You can ignore this one for hours before dinner. The caponata, an Italian mixed vegetable appetizer, gives it plenty of flavor.

1 onion
1½ lbs. beef chuck
1 (7½-oz.) can caponata
½ lb. mushrooms
½ tsp. salt
¼ tsp. freshly ground black pepper

Place a sheet of foil large enough to wrap around the meat in a square baking pan. Slice the onion and make a layer of slices on the foil. Place the meat on the onions and cover with the caponata. Distribute the mushrooms over the top. Sprinkle with salt and pepper. Bring the ends of the foil together and fold, making a tightly closed seam. Roll the sides up and crimp to prevent steam from escaping. Place in a 325° oven for 3 hours. Makes 4 servings.

Pozole Casserole

Pozole is a pork and hominy soup that you find in Mexico and California. Some claim it is a good morning-after remedy. I hope I have not limited its effectiveness by changing the pork to beef and transforming the soup into an equally tasty casserole.

1 long green chile
1 onion
1 clove garlic
1 tsp. salt
1 tbsp. butter
1 cup canned tomatoes, drained
½ tsp. oregano
¼ tsp. freshly ground black pepper
1 chorizo
1 lb. ground beef
1 (1-lb. 13-oz.) can hominy
1½ cups grated medium Tillamook cheese
¾ cup liquid from canned tomatoes

Place the chile under the broiler until it blisters and pops, then peel, seed, and chop it. Chop the onion. Mash the garlic in

½ teaspoon salt. Heat the butter in a skillet, add the onion and garlic and cook them until the onion is tender. Add the chile and the tomatoes. Crumble in the oregano and add the pepper. Simmer for 5 minutes.

Remove the casing from the chorizo and cook it in a large skillet until brown and crumbly. Lift the chorizo out of its drippings and set it aside. Brown the ground beef in the drippings, adding extra shortening if necessary. When the beef is browned, stir in the chorizo and ½ teaspoon salt.

Drain the hominy. (You will have about 3 cups.) In a 2-quart casserole, make a layer of one-third of the hominy. Top with one-third of the meat mixture and one-third of the onion-tomato mixture. Sprinkle with one-third of the grated cheese. Make 2 more layers in the same fashion, finishing with cheese. Pour the tomato liquid over the casserole and bake, uncovered, at 350° for 30–45 minutes. Makes 6 servings.

Lamb Chops Kasparian

We were discussing William Saroyan's novels when the conversation turned to food, and an Armenian friend gave me his favorite recipe for lamb chops.

4 lamb chops
Salt
Pepper
4 tsp. tomato paste
1 medium green pepper
1 onion
2 tomatoes

Lay the chops in a baking pan and sprinkle them with salt and pepper. Dot each chop with 1 teaspoon tomato paste. Cut the green pepper into strips. Chop the onion coarsely. Peel the tomatoes and cut them in eighths. Arrange the vegetables around the chops and bake, uncovered, at 350° for 1 hour. Turn the chops once. Makes 4 servings.

Pork Chops with Prunes and Wine

Pork takes to a sweet touch, in this case supplied by prunes and carrots. Boil or fry potatoes separately and you have the makings of a notable dinner.

    16 pitted prunes
     2 tbsp. sugar
     4 thick pork chops
       Salt
       Pepper
     1 onion
     6 carrots
    ½ cup liquid from plumping prunes
    ½ cup white wine
     1 tbsp. tomato purée
     1 tsp. red wine vinegar
       Pinch of marjoram
       Pinch of thyme

Place the prunes in a saucepan, covering them with hot water, and let them soak 2 hours. Simmer the prunes, covered, in the same liquid 2 hours, adding the sugar in the last ½ hour. Drain the prunes and reserve the liquid.

Trim some of the fat from the pork chops and melt it in a large skillet. Add the chops and brown them on each side. Season with salt and pepper to taste. Slice the onion and add it to the skillet. Cover and cook over low heat for ½ hour.

Meanwhile, scrape the carrots, cut them in 3-4 sections and slice the sections into strips. Parboil the strips in salted water for 10 minutes and drain.

Add the carrots, prunes, prune liquid, wine, tomato purée, and wine vinegar to the pork chops. Crumble in the marjoram and thyme and add another dash of salt. Cover and simmer 1 hour longer. Serve each chop with some of the sauce, carrots and prunes. Makes 4 servings.

Ginger Spareribs

Here is a typical Chinese treatment for spareribs. The marinade could be used as a barbecue baste, although these ribs are baked, and would be equally good with chicken. Fresh ginger and five spice powder give it a subtle perfume. If you don't have five spice powder, try a tiny pinch of anise.

    2 lbs. spareribs
    3 cloves garlic
    ½ tsp. salt
    1 tbsp. grated ginger root
    6 tbsp. soy sauce
    ⅓ cup sweet sherry
    3 tbsp. vinegar
    ⅓ cup sugar
    ½ tsp. Chinese five spice powder

Separate the ribs and place them in a baking pan. Mash the garlic cloves in the salt and combine them with the ginger root, soy sauce, sherry, vinegar, sugar, and five spice powder. Pour this marinade over the spareribs. Cover and refrigerate for 2 hours, turning the ribs occasionally in the marinade. Remove them from the refrigerator ½ hour before you cook them. Drain off most of the marinade and reserve. Bake the ribs, uncovered, at 350° for 1¼ hours, basting them with the reserved marinade and turning them as they brown. Makes 4 servings.

Shrimps Eric

This recipe comes from Spain, where the mashing of the sauce would be done in one of those wooden mortars that smell forever of garlic. The blender isn't so picturesque, but you'll never know the difference when you're eating these richly fragrant shrimp.

1½ lbs. medium shrimp
4 tbsp. butter
2 dozen blanched almonds
⅓ cup cracker crumbs
⅓ cup parsley
2 cloves garlic
1½ tsp. salt
1 cup plus 2 tbsp. dry white wine
1 onion

Shell and devein the shrimp and refrigerate them until needed. Melt 2 tablespoons butter in a small skillet and lightly brown the almonds. Stir in the cracker crumbs. Place the almonds, crumbs, parsley, 1 clove garlic, and ½ teaspoon salt in the blender. Add 2 tablespoons wine and blend until the mixture is coarsely puréed. It is all right if a few chunks of almond remain.

Mash the remaining clove of garlic in 1 teaspoon salt and chop the onion. In a large skillet, sauté the garlic and onion in the remaining 2 tablespoons butter until the onion is tender. Add 1 cup wine. When the wine comes to a boil, add the shrimp, and cook until pink (about 5 minutes). Stir in the almond mixture and simmer until very hot. If the sauce is too thick, thin it with a little more wine. Makes 4 servings.

Fish Steaks Mexican Style

In Mexico, they dress fish as decoratively as they do enchiladas. Here is a typical presentation featuring a red, white, and green chile-spiked sauce, freshened with lemon juice and finished off with cilantro sprigs.

1½ lbs. halibut steaks
4 tbsp. butter
Salt
Freshly ground pepper
1⅓ cups chopped onion (1 large onion)
1 clove garlic
2 long green chiles
1 (1-lb.) can stewed tomatoes

¼ tsp. oregano
⅛ tsp. ground cumin
4 tsp. lemon juice
   Cilantro sprigs

Wash the halibut and pat dry with paper towels. Line a baking
pan with aluminum foil, letting the foil extend up the sides of
the pan. Spread the foil with about 1 tablespoon softened butter.
Lay the halibut on the foil, dot with 2 tablespoons butter and
sprinkle with salt and pepper. Sprinkle ⅓ cup chopped onion over
the fish. Bake, uncovered, at 350° about 25 minutes, basting occasionally with the liquid which forms.
   Mash the garlic in ½ teaspoon salt. Heat the remaining 1 tablespoon butter in a skillet, add the garlic and remaining onion, and
cook them until the onion is tender. Add the chiles, which have
been peeled, seeded, and chopped, the tomatoes, oregano and
cumin. Simmer about 15 minutes. Divide the fish into 4 portions.
Top each with some of the sauce, sprinkle with 1 teaspoon lemon
juice and garnish with cilantro sprigs. Makes 4 servings.

Fish with Fresh Lime Sauce

   Limon means "lime" in Mexico, not lemon. I don't always get
the distinction straight, but I like what fresh "limon" does to fish.

2 lbs. lean white fish fillets
1 egg
1 cup cracker crumbs
6 tbsp. butter
1 medium onion
1 cup dry white wine
½–1 tsp. grated lime peel
   Juice of 1 large lime
   Few drops of hot pepper sauce
   Salt
   Freshly ground black pepper
   Pinch of sugar
   Lime slices
   Cilantro sprigs (optional)

Dip the fish in beaten egg, then in cracker crumbs, coating thoroughly. Line a baking pan with aluminum foil and butter the foil lightly. Place the fish on the foil and dot with 2 tablespoons butter. Bake at 350° 20 minutes, then brown under the broiler.

Meanwhile, chop the onion. Melt the remaining 4 tablespoons butter in a small saucepan. Add the onion and cook it until tender. Add the wine, lime peel and juice, hot pepper sauce, salt and pepper to taste, and sugar. Boil gently until the sauce reduces slightly. Serve the fish garnished with slices of lime and cilantro. Pass the sauce separately. Makes 4 servings.

Mexican Shells

If you want an outstanding company casserole, try this one. It is one of my favorites, full of the color and flavor with which the Mexicans seem to endow every dish. Don't be discouraged by the long list of ingredients. They go together quickly.

    1 medium onion
    2 tbsp. oil
    ¾ lb. ground beef
    2 chorizos
    ¼ cup chopped mild green chile
    1½ cups stewed tomatoes, drained
    1¼ cups liquid from tomatoes
    ⅓ cup tomato paste
    ⅓ cup red wine
    1 clove garlic
 1–1½ tsp. salt
    2 tsp. sugar
    ¼ tsp. freshly ground black pepper
    ½ tsp. oregano
    ¼ tsp. basil
    1 bay leaf
    1 (10-oz.) pkg. frozen spinach
    1 tbsp. butter
    ⅓ cup grated Parmesan cheese
    1 (10-oz.) pkg. shell macaroni
    1½ cups grated medium Tillamook cheese

Chop the onion and cook it until tender in 1 tablespoon oil in a heavy skillet. Lift the onion out and place it in a large saucepan. Add the remaining 1 tablespoon oil to the skillet and brown the beef, stirring to keep it crumbly. Add the beef to the onion. Remove the casing from the chorizos and cook them in the skillet until brown and crumbly. Lift them out of the drippings and add them to the beef. Now add the chile, tomatoes, tomato liquid, tomato paste, and wine to the saucepan. Crush the garlic in 1 teaspoon salt and add with the sugar and pepper. Crumble in the oregano and basil. Add the bay leaf. Simmer the sauce gently for 1–2 hours, then test to see if more salt is needed.

When ready to assemble the casserole, cook the spinach according to package directions and drain. Stir the butter and Parmesan cheese into the spinach.

Cook the macaroni shells in boiling salted water for 10–15 minutes, or until just tender. Drain.

Butter a large casserole. Make a layer of one-third of the shells. Top with one-third of the spinach mixture, spreading it evenly with your hands, and cover with some of the sauce. Make 2 more layers in this fashion finishing with the sauce. Sprinkle the Tillamook cheese over the top and bake the casserole, uncovered, at 350° 30–40 minutes, or until heated through and the cheese is bubbly. Pass additional grated Parmesan cheese, if desired. Makes 6 servings.

Wine Country Linguini

An honest Burgundy poured from the jug and a spicy chorizo make this sauce so good I could eat it without the pasta.

1 onion
1 clove garlic
1 tsp. salt
1–2 long green chiles
2 tbsp. butter
2 tbsp. olive oil
1 tbsp. flour
¾ lb. ground beef
1 chorizo
1 (8-oz.) can tomato sauce
1 (6-oz.) can tomato cocktail
6 tbsp. tomato paste
1 cup water
½ cup red wine
½ tsp. oregano
1 bay leaf
Pinch of cloves
1 tsp. sugar
¼ tsp. freshly ground black pepper
1 lb. linguini

Chop the onion and mash the garlic in ½ teaspoon salt. Place the chiles under the broiler until the skins blister and pop, then peel, seed, and mince them. Heat 1 tablespoon butter and 1 tablespoon olive oil in a skillet, add the onion, garlic, and chiles, and cook them until the onion is soft. Sprinkle with the flour and cook a little longer, stirring to blend. Place the onion mixture in a 3-quart saucepan.

Add the remaining olive oil and butter to the skillet and brown the beef, stirring to keep it crumbly. Add the beef to the saucepan. Remove the casing from the chorizo and cook it in the same skillet until brown and crumbly. Add the chorizo to the beef and onion. Now add the tomato sauce, tomato cocktail, tomato paste, water, and wine. Crumble in the oregano. Add the bay leaf, cloves, sugar, pepper, and remaining ½ teaspoon salt. Cover loosely and simmer gently 3 hours. Test for seasoning.

Cook the linguini in boiling salted water until tender. Drain it and serve it with the sauce poured over. If you do not use all the sauce at once, it freezes well. Makes 6 servings.

Baja Fettuccine

In Tijuana I encountered an excellent fettuccine with a new flavor. The secret? Canned milk.

¼ lb. thin noodles
3 tbsp. butter
⅓ cup freshly grated Parmesan cheese
1 (6-oz.) can evaporated milk
   Salt
   Freshly ground black pepper

Cook the noodles in boiling salted water until tender. Drain in a colander. Melt the butter in the pan in which the noodles were cooked. Return the noodles to the pan and toss with the butter, cheese, and milk. Add salt to taste and a generous sprinkling of black pepper. Toss again and serve with a little more pepper sprinkled over each serving. Makes 4 servings.

Eggplant Monterey

This eggplant recipe is nice in individual baking dishes, if you have them. That is the way it was served to me at an Italian restaurant on the Monterey Peninsula.

1 eggplant
   Olive oil
   Butter
   Medium Tillamook cheese
1 (1-lb.) can stewed tomatoes
½ tsp. oregano
½ tsp. basil
⅛ tsp. garlic powder
¼ cup freshly grated Parmesan cheese

Cut the eggplant in 8 slices and peel them. Heat 1 tablespoon olive oil and 1 tablespoon butter in a skillet. Add as many eggplant slices as can lie flat in the skillet and cook them until lightly browned on each side. Add more oil and butter as needed. Cut 8 long thin slices from a block of Tillamook cheese. In individual baking dishes or a large baking pan, lay out 1 slice of cheese for each serving. Fit 2 slices of eggplant together on top of the cheese. Drain the tomatoes and make a layer of tomatoes over the eggplant. Combine the oregano, basil, and garlic powder in a mortar and grind them as fine as possible. Sprinkle a pinch of the herbs over each serving of eggplant. Top with another slice of Tillamook cheese and sprinkle with 1 tablespoon Parmesan cheese. Bake at 350° for 15 minutes. Remove from the oven and sprinkle with the rest of the herb mixture. Makes 4 servings.

SANDWICHES

Sandwiches are informal foods, but now and then you find one that is a cut above the average and interesting enough to serve as the main dish for a luncheon. Here are two such sandwiches, one Danish and the other developed by a woman who was following a health food regime. I give the ingredients but no exact proportions, for sandwich makers should compose freely, without the restrictions of measuring cups and spoons. A bit more or less of one ingredient will have little effect upon the outcome.

Danish Salami Sandwich

I came across this open face sandwich at a restaurant called the Mollekroen in Solvang. There it was garnished with a strip of meat jelly. But since including the jelly would increase the preparation time for people like me from one minute to five hours, I leave it off. However, Knud Miller, the proprietor, suggested making the jelly by adding gelatin to canned consommé, coloring it with a little Kitchen Bouquet, and chilling it until firm.

Butter
Pumpernickel bread
Paper-thin slices of salami
Paper-thin slices of onion

For each sandwich, butter 2 slices of pumpernickel bread. (These are the narrow slices made by cutting a loaf-sized slice in half.) Line each slice of bread with 3–4 slices of salami, overlapping the salami and folding the bottom edges under to fit the slices more neatly on the bread. Cover with sliced onion. On the same plate, arrange a mound of potato salad in a lettuce leaf and add sliced tomato, cucumber, and ripe olives if you like.

Evelyn Long's Alfalfa Sprout Sandwich

I am not a vegetarian or a health food advocate, but neither am I interested in the reasoning behind a dish if the end result is good. And this sandwich is exceptionally tasty and attractive. The chia seed bread is made in Glendale, which is next door to Los Angeles, and the sandwich spread comes from Loma Linda, which has a plant in southern California.

Chia seed bread or whole wheat bread
Vegetarian sandwich spread
Mayonnaise
Alfalfa sprouts
Avocado slices
Seasoned salt
Turnip slices
Cherry tomatoes

For each serving, spread 1 slice of bread generously with the sandwich spread. Add a thin layer of mayonnaise and cover thickly with alfalfa sprouts. Top the sprouts with slices of avocado and sprinkle with seasoned salt. Garnish the plate with chilled turnip slices and peeled cherry tomatoes. To peel the tomatoes, immerse them in boiling water a few moments to loosen the skin.

6

Desserts

My book collection includes a strange little volume on nutrition written some fifty years ago by a woman doctor in Pasadena. Now Pasadena in those days was a vacation spot for the wealthy. The Santa Fe brought them West to inhabit rambling villas and to while away the months with genteel games of croquet on the lawns of the equally rambling old Huntington Hotel. But what use money when the delights it could purchase were not only sinful but positively poisonous? And the delights this little book sought to destroy were those of the table which, if you think about it, are the basis for all other pleasures. Nothing is quite so enjoyable without that well-fed sense of well-being that the patients of this scientific spoilsport must never have experienced.

Condiments, she wrote, were not only noxious but could cause corns in the stomach, while pickles pickled the interior, and highly seasoned food created a thirst that only alcohol could quench. Thus what we might call a passably good dinner would have sent a "pledge-signer" back to the saloon—not necessarily a bad fate if Pasadena had any exciting saloons in that era.

Alcohol, the destroyer of the race, was too vile to be discussed, wrote the doctor. But coffee, tea, and cocoa were not much better. And desserts—well, omit them from the diet and the body would not suffer for it. But in her chapter on sweets, this pleasure hater made one pithy comment that gets to the essence of the art of dessert making. The greatest chef, she observed, is he who can make a dessert so tempting that it appeals even to those who are already surfeited with food.

Of course, in a notoriously sweet-toothed nation such as the United States, this is not so hard to accomplish. Dessert to us is the elegant prize for having eaten our way through the rest of the meal like good little children. It alleviates not hunger but that eternal longing for something more, the desire for one more package under the Christmas tree. And the fancier that package the better. Not for us the gourmet's dessert of fresh fruit. What a bore! But values are relative, and the hothouse fruit that is treasured in one area rots on the ground in another.

When I can choose from cantaloupe, fresh pineapple, papayas, peaches, figs, grapefruit, bananas, strawberries, apples, pears, and grapes at any hour of the day for days on end, I am hardly going to be thrilled by more of the same for dinner. But in San Francisco during the Gold Rush, when apples cost as much as five dollars each, I would probably have tossed night after night with dreams of their juicy goodness.

I am presently tossing with dreams of the black raspberry dumplings of my childhood. It seems berries have become too expensive a crop for local growers, who have ripped out their vines and put in more profitable plants. I haven't seen black raspberries in the markets here for years. And I am afraid my hungering palate will have little influence over the growers' pocketbooks, which means I will have to plow up some grass and put in my own vines.

Those who like to ridicule Americans sometimes pick on their childlike addiction to sweets. Examine a cookbook compiled by a ladies' club and you will find at least half the book devoted to desserts, and usually the first half at that. Soups, meat, and vegetables are only afterthoughts.

But we have many facets of taste—sweet, sour, salty, and so forth. Can one be considered more or less worthy than another?

I do have one stand on desserts: I would rather have nothing than a disappointment. My first night in Paris I wandered alone into a café on the Champs Élysées. Devoid at that time of both language skills and a knowledgeable companion, I took the only safe course and ordered the prix fixe dinner.

The selection for dessert was an apricot tart—how deliciously French that sounded—or ice cream. Thinking of that perfunctory little scoop served so often in restaurants at home, I chose the tart. Only by the time I had finished my potage Faubonne, steak maître d'hôtel, pommes de terre frites and decanter of vin ordinaire, the tarts were gone. What a disaster!

But trust the French. They can't do anything in an ordinary fashion. They can't even scoop ice cream properly. What arrived was a twirled, spiraled, futuristic, absolutely mad creation of pink and green sherbets with a dainty wafer poised for takeoff on top.

My faith in ice cream was restored—even more so when I bought an electric freezer and began making my own combinations. You will find one of the best—a tantalizing tart-sweet citrus ice—in the recipes that follow.

Not only France but the entire world is full of culinary surprises. What is one man's dessert may be another man's salad or vegetable. In California, we use avocados primarily in dips and salads. But in Indonesia, they whip them with brandy or rum and sugar for an intriguing pudding. You will learn how to make that dessert in this chapter.

And beans—what else can one do but bake them, refry them, marinate them in a salad, or purée them into soup? But the Japanese use sweetened bean paste as a filling for pastries. And the Chinese combine mashed beans with dates and stuff other pastries with that. I often wander into the Oriental sections of Los Angeles to buy these confections. I find them quite interesting, although they are too much of a challenge for some of my friends.

In Mexico, I encountered a remarkable dessert called Dulce de Frijol Envinado, a mixture of puréed beans, milk, sugar, vanilla,

and sherry. Objectively, I would say the flavor was delicious—
rather like a poor man's zabaglione. But while eating it I felt not
poverty stricken but uneasy, as if I had doused apple pie with
ketchup.

Don't worry, the desserts in this chapter won't turn your taste
buds upside down. But they will take you along unfamiliar routes
and toss you from Cuba to Thailand in both directions around
the globe. For adventurers, there are oddities such as Japanese
cookies subtly flavored with powdered seaweed—probably the most
unlikely recipe in the lot.

If you recoil from that idea, you can try other cookies made
with akvavit or sesame seeds, the popular Chinese almond cookies,
or authentic French macaroons. You will also find a creamy rum
custard which is half Spanish and half French, an extraordinary
mango charlotte, a cloud-like Danish rice pudding with raspberry
sauce, and many other desserts that will make you the envy of
the cake-mix crowd.

I like to try the odd and exotic, but I never force the results on
anyone. My searches have taken me into the garage of an Australian
importer where I found passion fruit pulp (you need it for certain
Down Under desserts); into a market stall where a man from
Yucatan sold me a Mexican vanilla that makes other vanillas
taste like water; and into Cuban markets for chiviricos, bits of deep
fried, sugared dough that are nice for a snack.

My rarest dessert experiment involved sweet tamales flavored
with Cognac and lemon and wrapped in banana leaves. The
leaves would add a special flavor to the tamales, said the Ecua-
dorian lady who gave me the recipe, and I was not to substitute
corn husks or parchment paper.

In obtaining the leaves, I learned that anyone with a banana
tree in his yard is besieged by homesick Central Americans,
southern Mexicans, and certain South Americans, who all wrap
their tamales in the leaves. And I discovered one neighborhood
in downtown Los Angeles where all the trees had been preempted
by a Central American with a tamale shop.

At any rate, I wrapped my tamales in the banana leaves as
instructed and slipped in one wrapped in corn husks. After they
had steamed, came the unveiling. And with the concentration of
a Frenchman at his wines, I tasted back and forth between the

two versions. I suppose I shouldn't confess this, but I couldn't taste any difference. Does this mean that my palate is crippled? Or am I merely not a connoisseur of leaves?

Mango Rum Charlotte

A spectacular dessert, this pale, golden charlotte reflects the constant sun that attracts so many people to southern California. The mangoes add a tropical taste appropriate to our palm trees, banana trees, and sometimes overly tropical weather.

> 1 (15-oz.) can sliced mangoes
> 2 eggs, separated
> ¼ cup sugar
> 2 tbsp. lemon juice
> Dash of salt
> 1 env. unflavored gelatin
> ¼ cup syrup from canned mangoes
> 3 tbsp. rum
> 1 tbsp. orange Curaçao
> 1½ cups heavy cream
> 1 pkg. ladyfingers

Drain the mangoes, reserving ¼ cup syrup. (You should have about 1 cup mangoes.) Reserve a few slices for garnish and purée the remainder through a sieve. Beat the egg yolks and add them to the mangoes with the sugar, lemon juice, and salt. Soften the gelatin in the reserved syrup. Cook and stir the mango mixture in the top of a double boiler over simmering water until warm. Add the gelatin and cook and stir until the gelatin is dissolved and the mixture coats a wooden spoon. Cool until the mixture begins to set. Add the rum and Curaçao. Beat the egg whites until stiff and fold in. Whip 1 cup cream until stiff and fold into the mixture.

Split the ladyfingers, measure them against the side of a 9-inch spring-form pan and trim them even with the top of the pan. Dip the ladyfingers in a saucer of rum and line them vertically around the side of the pan. Pour in the mango mixture, smooth the surface, and chill. Before serving, whip the remaining ½ cup cream and flavor with a little Curaçao. Smooth the cream over the mango mixture. Arrange the reserved mango slices in the center. Place the dessert on a serving platter and carefully remove the sides of the pan. Makes 6 servings.

California Dried Fruit Compote

California produces multitudes of prunes and raisins, which taste even more delicious when cooked in another of our famous products, wine.

  2 cups prunes (about 20 prunes)
  1 cup hot water
1½ cups dry red wine
  ¼ cup golden raisins
  1 stick cinnamon
  3 whole cloves
  ¾ cup granulated sugar
  ½ (3-oz.) pkg. cream cheese
  ½ tsp. grated orange peel
  ½ tsp. grated lemon peel
  1 tbsp. powdered sugar
  ½ cup heavy cream

Put the prunes to soak overnight in 1 cup hot water and ½ cup wine. The next day, add the remaining 1 cup wine, the raisins, cinnamon stick, and cloves. Bring to a boil, then simmer, loosely covered, over low heat for 30 minutes. Add the granulated sugar, stir and simmer 10 minutes longer, or until the prunes are puffed and tender. Strain the liquid from the prunes and boil it until it reduces a little and becomes syrupy. Pour the syrup over the prunes and raisins, cool, and then chill.

Work the cream cheese with a fork until softened. Blend in the orange and lemon peels and the powdered sugar. Add the cream gradually, beating with the fork until smooth. Then beat with a rotary beater until stiff. Chill. Top each serving with a mound of the flavored cream. Makes 4 servings.

Spanish Orange Cream

Many old California families trace their genealogy to Spain. The same country produced this coolly elegant party mold flavored with orange and sherry.

⅓ cup mixed candied pineapple and orange peel
1½ tbsp. orange Curaçao
2 egg yolks
3 tbsp. sugar
   Pinch of salt
1 tsp. grated orange peel
5 tbsp. medium sweet sherry
1 tsp. unflavored gelatin
2 tbsp. water
⅔ cup heavy cream
   Chopped toasted almonds (optional)

Chop the pineapple and orange peel in small pieces and soak them in the Curaçao. In the top of a double boiler beat the egg yolks with the sugar, salt, and grated orange peel. Add the sherry. Place over simmering water and beat with a rotary beater until the mixture foams and rises. Soften the gelatin in the water, add to the egg mixture, and continue beating until the gelatin is dissolved and the mixture slightly thickened. Let cool, stirring occasionally.

Whip the cream until stiff and fold into the cooled mixture. Fold in the candied fruits. Pour into a 1-quart mold, smooth the surface, and freeze. Remove from the freezer and place in the refrigerator about 1 hour before serving. Unmold and sprinkle with chopped toasted almonds if desired. Makes 4 servings.

Tacos de Cajeta

The taco is a way of life in southern California. You can't drive a mile without passing a taco stand, and supermarkets sell the crisp, fried tortilla shells into which you can pack your own beef, tomatoes, lettuce, and cheese. But dessert tacos are something else. In this recipe, the taco shells are actually crepes and the filling is the caramel-like cajeta, the recipe for which you will find in the chapter on "The Flavor of Mexico."

THE TACO SHELLS (CREPES):

⅔ cup instantized flour

2 tsp. sugar

Pinch of salt

⅛ tsp. cinnamon

2 eggs

½ cup milk

½ cup water

1 tbsp. melted butter

THE FILLING:

1 cup cajeta (see page 183)

⅔ cup shredded coconut

2 tbsp. butter

2 tsp. sugar

6 tbsp. rum

To make the taco shells, combine the flour, sugar, salt, and cinnamon. Beat the eggs and add to them the milk, water, and butter. Add the dry ingredients and beat until smooth. Heat a 7-inch skillet and brush it with a little butter. Pour in 2 tablespoons of the batter and tilt the pan to spread the batter evenly. Cook until the taco is set, then turn and cook a minute or so on the other side. Continue making tacos in this fashion until the batter is used up. Pile them on a plate and cover with waxed paper until you are ready to use them. You will have 12–14 tacos.

To make the filling, combine the cajeta and coconut. If the cajeta is too stiff, thin it with a little rum or sherry. Place a generous tablespoonful of filling on each taco. Roll up and place side by side on an ovenproof platter. If you are making the tacos in advance, you can now cover and refrigerate them.

To serve, melt the 2 tablespoons butter and pour over the tacos. Sprinkle with the sugar and place in a 350° oven for 10 minutes, or until heated through. Pour the rum over and flame at the table. Makes 6 servings of 2 tacos each.

Mexican Citrus Ice

Sharp, clean, and refreshing, this ice is a modernization of an old Mexican recipe, the only change being the use of frozen juice when the fresh is out of season. In hot weather you will find its bright blend of flavors irresistible. It is also ideal after a spicy Mexican or Italian dinner.

4½ cups water
1 cinnamon stick
2 whole cloves
   Peel of ½ orange
   Peel of ½ lemon
1 cup sugar
1 env. unflavored gelatin
3 tbsp. water
   Juice of 4 oranges
   Juice of 2 lemons
1 (6-oz.) can frozen concentrated tangerine juice
¾ cup dry white wine
⅓ cup rum

In a saucepan, combine the 4½ cups water, cinnamon stick, cloves, orange and lemon peels, and sugar. Bring to a boil. Meanwhile, soften the gelatin in the 3 tablespoons water. Add the gelatin to the boiling liquid, stirring until dissolved. Remove from heat and steep, covered, for 1 hour. Strain the liquid. Add the orange, lemon, and tangerine juices, wine, and rum. Pour into an ice cream freezer container, surround with ice and salt, and freeze. Makes about 3 pints.

NOTE: I made this ice once in the freezing compartment of the refrigerator, beating the mixture as it froze. The texture was not as good as with the ice cream freezer, but the flavor was delicious.

Tropical Mousse

This frozen mousse is based on a Los Angeles recipe of a few decades ago. The macadamia nuts that garnish it are a specialty of Hawaii, but macadamia trees are also cultivated in southern California, and a few grow on the streets of Beverly Hills.

¾ cup canned crushed pineapple
⅓ cup syrup from canned pineapple
2 egg yolks
   Pinch of salt
⅓ cup sugar
¼ tsp. grated lime peel
1 tbsp. lime juice
½ cup heavy cream
1 tbsp. powdered sugar
2 tbsp. chopped candied ginger
   Chopped macadamia nuts or chopped toasted almonds

Drain the pineapple. Beat the pineapple syrup, egg yolks, and salt together in the top of a double boiler. Cook over simmering water, stirring constantly, until the yolks are cooked and the mixture thickens. Add the pineapple, sugar, lime peel, and juice. Stir to blend and cool. Whip the cream until stiff and fold in the sifted powdered sugar. Add the ginger to the pineapple mixture and fold into the whipped cream. Turn into a 1-quart mold and place in the freezer. When the mixture has begun to freeze around the edges, beat it with a fork. Return it to the freezer. Beat once more, then freeze until firm. Unmold and sprinkle with chopped macadamia nuts. Makes 4 servings.

Rødgrod med Fløde
(*Danish Red Pudding with Cream*)

The name of this dessert is possibly the most difficult phrase to pronounce in the Danish language. I am half Danish and wouldn't attempt it, but I do like the rich fruitiness and deep red

color of this famous Scandinavian dessert. Don't add too much
sugar, for it should be tart. Since the pudding is thickened with
cornstarch, it won't acquire the firm set of a gelatin dessert and
may turn out almost firm or moderately soupy depending upon
the juiciness of the fruits. I find it equally good either way. The
combination of rhubarb and strawberries was suggested by my
completely Danish Aunt Helen, who lives in Sacramento.

¾ lb. trimmed rhubarb
2 cups water
1 (10-oz.) pkg. frozen strawberries
1 (10-oz.) pkg. frozen raspberries
½ cup sugar or more to taste
2 tsp. lemon juice
6 tbsp. cornstarch
Sliced blanched almonds
Whipped cream

Cut the trimmed rhubarb into ½-inch chunks. (You should have
2–2½ cups chunks.) Place the rhubarb and water in a 2-quart
saucepan. Cook until the rhubarb is very tender. Add the strawberries and raspberries and cook them until thawed. Strain the
mixture through a sieve, pressing out as much juice from the fruit
as possible. (You will have approximately 4¾ cups juice.) Stir
in the sugar and lemon juice. Let the mixture cool slightly. Add
a little of the cooled juice to the cornstarch and stir until smooth.
Return the cornstarch mixture to the juice, mixing thoroughly.
Bring to a boil, stirring constantly. Boil and stir about 5 minutes,
or until the mixture thickens. Pour into a 2-quart casserole that
has been rinsed with hot water. Let the pudding cool, then chill
it. The pudding will stiffen as it cools. Arrange the sliced almonds
in a pattern over the surface. Top each serving with whipped
cream. Makes about 10 servings.

Ris à l'Amande with Rum and Raspberry Sauce

I fell in love with Scandinavian rice puddings while traveling
to the Orient on Norwegian freighters. This version is Danish

and as fluffy as the clouds I used to watch scudding over the Pacific.

2 cups milk
¼ cup rice
Pinch of salt
1 env. unflavored gelatin
¼ cup cold water
5 tbsp. sugar
1 tsp. vanilla
5 tbsp. chopped blanched almonds
¼ cup rum
1½ cups heavy cream
Sliced almonds for garnish

RASPBERRY SAUCE:
1 (10-oz.) pkg. frozen raspberries
1 tbsp. sugar
1½ tsp. cornstarch
2 tbsp. rum

Bring the milk to a boil in a saucepan. Add the rice and salt and stir with a fork. Cook, uncovered, over very low heat until the rice has absorbed most of the milk and the mixture is thick, about 1 hour and 15 minutes. Stir occasionally and watch that the mixture does not stick to the pan and burn.

Soften the gelatin in the cold water and dissolve over hot water. Stir the gelatin into the hot rice mixture and add the sugar, vanilla, almonds, and rum. Let cool. Whip 1 cup of cream until stiff and fold the cooled rice mixture into the cream. Pour into a greased 1-quart mold and chill until firm.

Meanwhile, make the sauce. Thaw the raspberries, pour about 2 tablespoons of the juice into a custard cup and put the remaining juice and berries through a sieve, discarding the seeds. Stir the sugar into the purée. Dissolve the cornstarch in the reserved juice and stir into the purée. Cook and stir over moderate heat until the sauce clears, comes to a boil, and thickens. Cool, then chill. Do not add the rum until just before serving.

To serve the dessert, dip the mold into hot water for a few seconds, work carefully around the edge with a small, sharp knife, and invert on a serving dish. Whip the remaining ½ cup cream until stiff and frost the top and sides of the dessert with the cream. Stud with sliced almonds and place a dab of sauce in the center. Stir the 2 tablespoons rum into the remaining sauce and pass separately with the pudding. Makes 6 servings.

Danish Apple Cake

If you're tired of apple pie, why not try apple cake? A Danish hall in Los Angeles serves it this way, with a touch of almond flavoring.

2 large apples
½ cup water
3 tbsp. plus 1 tsp. sugar
3 tbsp. butter
⅔ cup fine Melba toast crumbs (about 14 slices)
¼ cup crumbled almond paste
Cinnamon
⅔ cup heavy cream
¼ tsp. almond extract

Cut the apples in eighths. Remove the stems and blossom ends but do not peel or core. Place the apples in a saucepan with the water. Cover and boil until tender, about ½ hour. Purée the apples through a food mill or sieve and stir in 3 tablespoons sugar.

Melt the butter in a small skillet. Stir in the crumbs and 1 teaspoon sugar. Add the almond paste. Press the paste against the pan with the back of a spoon to soften it and blend it with the crumbs.

In a small baking dish or casserole, make a layer of half the applesauce. Top with half the crumbs. Add the remaining applesauce and top with the remaining crumbs. Dust lightly with cinnamon. Bake at 350° for 20 minutes. Whip the cream with the almond extract. Serve the cake warm topped with whipped cream and dusted with more cinnamon. Makes 4 servings.

Albert's Swiss Apple Pie

"As American as apple pie" goes the saying, but this apple pie is Swiss, modeled after one made by the chef at a ski lodge in New Mexico. The chef was not only Swiss but a terrific skier. And the pie testifies to his good taste. One of my friends bit into a slice and thought she was eating baklava, the Turkish pastry. Another asked if it were mince pie. That is the double effect you get from the chopped nuts and raisins that line the pie shell.

1 9-in. unbaked pie shell
2 eggs
¾ cup plus 1 tbsp. sugar (vary with tartness of apples)
1 cup milk
   Pinch of salt
¼ tsp. vanilla
3 large apples
2 tsp. lemon juice
¼ tsp. cinnamon
½ cup finely chopped walnuts
⅓ cup seedless raisins
   Pinch of ground cinnamon mixed with 1 tsp. sugar

Prepare the pie shell according to your favorite recipe and place it in the refrigerator until ready to use. Beat the eggs until foamy. Add 5 tablespoons sugar, the milk, salt, and vanilla and beat well. Cut the apples into quarters. Peel, core, and grate them. Toss the apples with the lemon juice and then with the remaining ½ cup sugar and ¼ teaspoon cinnamon. (It won't matter if the apples turn brown, but I prepare them last in hopes that they won't.)

Cover the pie shell with a layer of nuts and scatter the raisins evenly over the nuts. Add the apples and spread them evenly over the shell. Pour in the egg mixture and sprinkle with the cinnamon and sugar. Bake at 350° for 1 hour, or until the custard is set. Serve warm.

French Rum Cream

One book has been written about the history of the French in Los Angeles, and another could be done about their contributions to the California wine industry. That makes this creamy French pudding at home here. Coated with caramel as are the Spanish flans, it blends two aspects of our culture.

      2 cups milk
      1 cup half-and-half
      1 strip lemon peel
      1 cup less 1 tbsp. sugar
    5½ tbsp. butter
      ⅓ cup flour
      ¼ tsp. grated lemon peel
        Pinch salt
      3 tbsp. rum
      4 eggs, separated

CARAMEL SAUCE:
      1 cup sugar
      1 cup water

Combine the milk, half-and-half, lemon peel, and 7 tbsp. sugar in a saucepan and bring to a boil. Melt the butter in another saucepan and stir in the flour until smooth. Add the boiling liquid, stirring to prevent lumps. Remove the lemon peel. When thoroughly blended, remove the milk mixture from heat. Add the grated lemon peel, salt, and rum. Let the mixture cool slightly, stirring occasionally to prevent a skin from forming on the top. Beat the egg yolks and add. Beat the egg whites until stiff. Fold the mixture into the egg whites and beat to remove lumps.

Melt the remaining ½ cup sugar in a small saucepan and cook until golden brown. Pour the caramel little by little into a 2-quart casserole and spread over the bottom. Pour the pudding mixture into the casserole. Place in a pan of hot water and bake at 350° for 1 hour, or until a knife inserted in the center comes out clean. Plan the pudding to be finished about 1 hour before serving time so it will still be warm.

To make the sauce, place the sugar in a saucepan and heat, stirring constantly, until it melts. Then cook until a rich brown. Add the water very slowly, for it will spatter. Cook the sauce over low heat until blended. Serve either warm or cold.

Loosen the pudding around the top with a small knife. Invert on a serving dish and accompany with the Caramel Sauce. Makes 6 servings.

Peach Clafoutis

You don't need a mix to make an easy dessert. This clafoutis, a classic French country dish, is handy when guests come to dinner on short notice. You will like the combination of peaches with the delicate, almond-flavored topping.

    8 canned peach halves
    ¼ cup sugar
    3 tbsp. brandy
    2 tbsp. butter
    2 eggs
    5 tbsp. flour
    ⅛ tsp. salt
    1½ cups milk
    ¼ tsp. almond extract
    ½ tsp. vanilla

Drain the peach halves, cut each in 4 pieces and place them in a wide, shallow casserole. Sprinkle with 2 tablespoons sugar and the brandy and dot with the butter. In a mixing bowl, beat the eggs, add the remaining 2 tablespoons sugar, and sift in the flour and salt. Add the milk, almond extract, and vanilla and beat thoroughly. Pour this batter, which will be quite thin, over the peaches. Bake, uncovered, at 350° for 30-45 minutes, or until lightly browned. Makes 6 servings.

Coeur à la Crème with Strawberry-Port Sauce

Much of my "French" cooking equipment is made in Japan, including the perforated heart-shaped molds which are traditional for this dessert. (For easier unmolding, line the molds with a dampened double thickness of cheesecloth). You will find it a pleasant change from ice cream with a fruit topping.

1½ cups cottage cheese
1 (3-oz.) pkg. cream cheese
½ cup heavy cream
1 tbsp. powdered sugar
1 tsp. vanilla

STRAWBERRY-PORT SAUCE:

1 (10-oz.) pkg. frozen strawberries
1 tsp. lemon juice
1 tbsp. cornstarch
¼ cup port

Put the cottage cheese through a sieve into a mixing bowl. Add the softened cream cheese, cream, sugar, and vanilla and beat with an electric beater until fluffy and smooth. Pack into 6 perforated individual heart-shaped molds or 1 large one. Place on a platter to catch any drips and chill for several hours or overnight.

Thaw the strawberries and drain the juice into a small saucepan. Add the lemon juice. Blend the cornstarch with the port and add to the juice. Bring the mixture to a boil and cook until thickened. Add the strawberries to the sauce and chill.

Run a small knife around each mold and turn out on dessert plates. Pour some of the sauce over each. Makes 6 servings.

Almond Curd with Fresh Coconut

This dessert migrated across the Pacific. The almond-flavored gelatin is typically Chinese and the coconut topping was added in Hawaii.

1 tbsp. (1 env.) plus 1 tsp. unflavored gelatin
2 cups half-and-half
¼ cup granulated sugar
⅛ tsp. salt
2 tbsp. rum
½ tsp. almond extract
2 cups grated fresh coconut
⅓ cup powdered sugar
½ cup toasted sliced almonds

Soften the gelatin in ½ cup of the half-and-half. In a saucepan combine the remaining half-and-half, the granulated sugar and salt. Heat slowly. Add the gelatin mixture and stir constantly until dissolved. Bring the mixture just to the boil. Remove from heat and stir in the rum and almond extract. Pour into a 1-quart pyrex loaf pan or other rectangular mold. Cool, then chill until firm. Toss the coconut with the powdered sugar. Cut the gelatin into squares, top each with a generous amount of coconut and sprinkle with toasted almonds. Makes 6 servings.

Sweet Beads

I've had some excellent Chinese meals on the high seas. To explain, the ship on which I sailed from Yokohama to Los Angeles was staffed with Chinese cooks from Hong Kong. This unusual dessert ended one of their dinners. The beads are really tapioca, the largest you can get.

½ cup large pearl tapioca
   Dash of salt
4 canned pear halves

CHOCOLATE SAUCE:
3 oz. semi-sweet chocolate
3 tbsp. coffee
5 tbsp. half-and-half
1½ tsp. butter
   Dash of salt
2 tbsp. rum
   Chopped toasted almonds

Soak the tapioca in water to cover generously for 3 hours. Add a dash of salt and simmer until the tapioca is transparent. Drain, rinse with cold water, and chill. Chill the pear halves.

Melt the chocolate in a small saucepan. Stir in the coffee by tablespoons, then add the half-and-half, butter, and salt. Stir to blend. Remove from heat, add the rum, and let cool.

For each serving, fill the center of a pear half with a spoonful of the tapioca. Cover generously with chocolate sauce and sprinkle with almonds. Makes 4 servings.

Minted Longans

Chinatown dinners end with simple sweets such as almond cookies, fortune cookies, or a plate of fruits that might include lychees, longans, kumquats, and pineapple. A little more elaborate is this dessert of pineapple-stuffed longans atop a Crème de Menthe frappe. The stuffed longans are imported canned from Taiwan. If you can't get them, substitute pineapple chunks and any other fruit you like with mint.

For each serving allow:

6 pineapple-stuffed longans
2 or 3 cubes green ice
1 tbsp. green Crème de Menthe

Drain the longans and chill them. (I buy them in a 20-oz. can that provides about 8 servings.) Tint water emerald green with a few drops of green food color and freeze in ice cube trays. Assemble the dessert in stemmed dessert glasses. Crush the ice and place a bed of ice in each glass. Pour over the Crème de Menthe and top with the longans. Accompany with crisp cookies.

Chinatown Coconut Candy

The sugary chips of coconut sold in Chinese pastry shops are surprisingly easy to make. I like my mother's technique with a coconut. She punctures the softest eye, drains out the milk, then

cracks the nut by throwing it with all her might on the driveway.
This is her recipe.

1 coconut
1 cup granulated sugar
¾ cup water
  Powdered sugar

Puncture the softest eye of the coconut and drain out the milk.
Crack the shell, cut out the meat, and peel off the thin brown
skin attached to it. Cut the meat in thin slices. Bring the granulated sugar and water to a boil. Add the coconut slices and cook
gently, uncovered, for 2–3 hours, or until most of the syrup is
absorbed. Cover a sheet of waxed paper with sifted powdered
sugar. Lay the drained coconut slices on the sugar, cover them
with more powdered sugar, and toss with a fork until the coconut
slices are thoroughly coated with sugar. Cool and store in an
airtight container.

Gula Malacca

The Cockpit Hotel in Singapore is famous for its Indonesian
rijsttafel luncheons. The incredible parade of foods, carried in by
Malay boys clad in batik, ends with this tapioca dessert. You eat
it with two sauces, one of coconut cream, the other of melted
gula malacca, which is palm sugar. Since gula malacca isn't available in Los Angeles, I base my sauce on the golden syrup that
comes from England. It produces the same effect—a thin syrup
with a faint molasses flavor.

2 cups plus 2 tbsp. milk
5 tbsp. quick-cooking tapioca
1 tbsp. sugar
Dash of salt

COCONUT CREAM:
1 cup half-and-half
¼ cup packaged shredded coconut
1 tbsp. sugar

GOLDEN SAUCE:
½ cup golden syrup
2 tbsp. water
½–1 tsp. molasses

Combine the milk, tapioca, sugar, and salt in a saucepan and let stand for 5 minutes. Bring to a boil and cook for 1 minute, or until very thick. Pour into custard cups or ramekins of about ½ cup capacity. Cool, then chill until firm.

To make the coconut cream, combine the half-and-half, coconut, and sugar and bring to a boil. Remove from heat and let steep, covered, for 1 hour. Strain the cream, pressing out as much juice as possible from the coconut. Chill.

Combine the golden syrup, water, and molasses in a small saucepan and heat, stirring until blended. Serve this sauce at room temperature.

At serving time, turn the molds of tapioca out into small dessert bowls. (Running a knife around the edge will help to loosen them.) Pass the sauces in separate pitchers and pour some of each over the tapioca. Makes 4–5 servings.

Vermicelli Sorn Daeng

The steamy climate of Bangkok requires antidotes such as this chilly dessert, which is the most novel treatment of pasta I've encountered. The vermicelli in its icy coconut soup cooled me off after a spicy curry at the Sorn Daeng, a Thai restaurant where the air conditioning consisted of breezes wafting through latticed walls.

2 cups half-and-half
½ cup packaged shredded coconut
¼ cup sugar
2 oz. vermicelli (about 1½ coils)
1 tbsp. oil
4–5 ice cubes
   Rose syrup

Combine the half-and-half, coconut, and sugar in a saucepan and bring just to a boil. Remove from heat, cover, and let steep 1 hour. Strain the mixture, pressing out as much liquid as possible from the coconut. Cool, then chill. (If you are serving curry before this dessert, toast the coconut, and use it as a sambal.)

Break the vermicelli into 2–3-inch lengths. Bring a generous amount of water to a boil, add the oil and vermicelli, and cook for 8 minutes, or until the vermicelli is tender. Drain and rinse with cold water.

Divide the vermicelli among four dessert bowls. Add to each ½ cup of the coconut cream. Crack the ice and divide it among the bowls. Then add 2 teaspoons rose syrup to each serving. Makes 4 servings.

NOTE: Raspberry, boysenberry, or other red fruit syrup may be substituted for the rose syrup.

Avocados Soeleiman

Ann Soeleiman brought out a mixing bowl and an avocado and showed me how to make this Indonesian dessert. I serve it in wine glasses with small, shallow bowls that are too little for wine but just right for a first taste of this exotic pudding.

1 large, very ripe avocado
2 tbsp. sugar or more to taste
2 tbsp. cream
1 tbsp. rum
   Few grains salt
   Shredded coconut

Peel the avocado and mash it with a fork until smooth. Blend in the sugar, cream, rum, and salt. Cover and chill. Serve in small stemmed glasses and garnish with coconut. Makes 4 small servings.

Orange Shells with Native Cheese

One of my favorite dinners in Puerto Rico featured black bean soup, the rice and chicken dish called asopao, and orange shells with native cheese. The shells are good as they come from the can but considerably better when touched up as in the following recipe. Although Puerto Rican native cheese is available in Los Angeles, I use Teleme, a native California cheese. Both are pale yellow and bland. You can also serve cream cheese with this dessert.

    1 (1-lb. 2-oz.) can orange shells
      Grated peel of ½ orange
      Juice of 1 orange
    2 tsp. lemon juice
    4 slices Teleme cheese

Place the orange shells and their syrup in a saucepan. Add the orange peel and orange juice and bring to a boil. When the mixture has boiled briefly, add the lemon juice. Remove from heat, cool, then chill. Serve the shells in small bowls with a generous amount of syrup and a slice of cheese. Makes 4 servings.

Dulce de Coco
(Coconut Dessert)

The Pan American Restaurant in Los Angeles introduced me to Cuban desserts, including this unusual combination of cream cheese with a syrupy coconut topping. Any leftover topping will keep almost indefinitely in the refrigerator and can be used in many ways. I add a little to tropical drinks that I make in the blender. You can also serve it over fresh fruit or ice cream.

3 cups grated fresh coconut
3 cups sugar
3 cups water
¼ cup light corn syrup
½ tsp. coconut extract
1 (8-oz.) pkg. cream cheese

To prepare the coconut meat, puncture the softest eye of the coconut shell, drain out the milk, and crack the shell. Pry out the meat and cut off the thin brown skin attached to it. Grate the meat and pack it down when measuring.

Combine the sugar, water, and corn syrup in a large saucepan and bring to a boil. Add the coconut and boil gently, stirring frequently, for 1¼ hours, or until very thick. Remove from heat and stir in the coconut extract. Cool and refrigerate. You will have about 1 quart topping.

Divide the cream cheese into eight slices. Top each slice with a generous amount of the coconut mixture. Makes 8 servings.

NOTE: If you like lots of syrup, boil 1 cup water with 1 cup sugar and 2 tablespoons light corn syrup to a temperature of 220° on a candy thermometer. Flavor with a few drops of coconut extract and add as desired to each serving of dessert.

Cuban Bananas in Wine

Cubans serve these bananas as a meat accompaniment, but I like them for dessert.

4 large bananas
¼ cup butter
⅔ cup brown sugar
⅔ cup red wine
1 small piece cinnamon stick
1 tsp. grated orange peel

Peel the bananas. Cut them in half crosswise and again length-wise. Melt the butter in a skillet, add the bananas, and cook them until softened. Sprinkle the bananas with the sugar and cook until the sugar melts. Add the wine, cinnamon stick, and orange peel. Boil gently until the wine reduces and forms a thick syrup. Let the bananas cool slightly in the syrup and serve them while still warm. Makes 4 servings.

Great House Banana Fritters

Jack and Annette Gold retired to southern California, found life here too hectic, and escaped to Jamaica. An advertisement in a Los Angeles newspaper led them to buy a crumbling mansion at Sign near Montego Bay. With the house they acquired a superb Jamaican cook. And the restored Great House at Sign is now a delightful inn where native foods are served in a setting reminiscent of leisurely plantation days. These banana fritters ended luncheon the day I visited the Golds. The Jamaican girl who served them gave me the recipe.

    1 banana
    1 egg
    ½ tsp. sugar
    ¼ tsp. vanilla
    2 tbsp. milk
    1 tbsp. flour
      Dash of salt
    1–2 tbsp. butter
      Raw sugar
    1 lime

Mash the banana thoroughly with a fork and add the well-beaten egg, sugar, vanilla, milk, flour, and salt. Mix well. Melt the butter in a skillet and add the batter by spoonfuls, forming fritters approximately 3 inches in diameter. Cook until golden brown on each side. Serve the fritters folded in half, sprinkled with raw sugar and a few drops of lime juice. Makes about 10 fritters.

Peaches with Orange Sherry Cream

A warm, winey sauce that is really a form of zabaglione makes a wonderful topping for fresh peaches. Don't try this recipe in large quantities. It might foam right out of your double boiler.

2 peaches
1 tbsp. peach brandy
2 egg yolks
3 tbsp. sugar
5 tbsp. dry sherry
1 tbsp. orange Curaçao

Peel and slice the peaches and sprinkle them lightly with sugar. Divide them into 3 servings and pour 1 teaspoon peach brandy over each.

In the top of a double boiler, beat the egg yolks with the 3 tablespoons sugar, sherry, and Curaçao. Place over simmering water and continue to beat with a rotary beater until the mixture foams, rises, and clings to the beater when you lift it. Pour over the peaches and serve immediately. Makes 3 servings.

Orange Omelet Flambé

A tiny Irish import shop yielded the crock of Dublin marmalade that inspired this puffy omelet. As a variation you can substitute strawberry jam without changing the rest of the ingredients.

2 eggs, separated
1 tbsp. plus 1 tsp. powdered sugar
1 tbsp. cream
1 tsp. orange Curaçao
1 tsp. grated orange peel
Pinch of salt
Butter
1 tbsp. orange marmalade
1 jigger rum

Break the egg yolks into a small bowl and add 1 tablespoon powdered sugar, the cream, Curaçao, ½ teaspoon grated orange peel, and salt. Beat the egg whites until stiff but not dry. With the same beater, beat the egg yolks until foamy. Fold the yolk mixture into the whites. Heat a little butter in a small skillet until very hot. (I use a non-stick pan and about 2 teaspoons butter.) Pour the egg mixture in and lower the heat to moderate. Let cook until the bottom is set and lightly browned. Spread the marmalade along the omelet to one side of the center. Fold the omelet in half. If it should tear as you fold, push it together with a spatula and it will hold its shape. Cook briefly on each side, then, with wide spatulas, lift onto a warmed serving platter. Brush with a little melted butter, sprinkle with the remaining teaspoon powdered sugar and ½ teaspoon grated orange peel. Pour the rum over and flame. Makes 2 servings.

Brentwood Apricot Squares

Brentwood, Bel-Air, and Pacific Palisades are luxury residential areas between Los Angeles and the ocean. In one of the smart neighborhood shopping centers I found rare wines, imported groceries, and a bakery featuring these pastries.

1 cup flour
½ cup butter
1 (3-oz.) pkg. cream cheese
Apricot jam
Powdered sugar

Place the flour in a mixing bowl. Cut in the butter, work in the softened cream cheese, and mix thoroughly. Form the dough into a ball. Divide in half and roll each half out on a floured board until ⅛-inch thick. Cut into 3-inch squares. Place a spoonful of apricot jam on each square. Fold each corner toward the center, but do not bring the corners together, for you want some of the filling to show. Bake at 375° about 10 minutes, or until lightly browned. Sprinkle a sheet of waxed paper with powdered sugar.

Set the pastries on the sugar and sprinkle them with additional powdered sugar. Makes about 20 pastries.

Sesame Crisps

Sesame seeds and the richly perfumed sesame oil sold in Oriental markets combine in an excellent cooky.

    3 tbsp. butter
    ½ cup sugar
    1 egg, separated
    1 tbsp. sesame oil
    1 tbsp. rum
    1½ tsp. cream
    ½ tsp. vanilla
    ¾ cup flour
    ½ tsp. baking powder
    ¼ tsp. salt
      Toasted sesame seeds

Cream the butter with the sugar. Beat in the egg yolk and add the sesame oil, rum, cream, and vanilla. Sift in the flour, baking powder, and salt. Form the dough into a roll, wrap in waxed paper, and chill overnight. Slice into cookies about ⅛-inch thick. Brush the top of each cooky with egg white and sprinkle with toasted sesame seeds. Bake at 375° for 8–10 minutes, or until lightly browned. Makes 3½ dozen small cookies.

Japanese Tea Cookies

Seaweed sounds like a terrible ingredient for cookies. But aonoriko, or powdered seaweed, looks like any flaky, green herb and adds an interesting depth of flavor to this recipe. If the idea appalls you, leave out the seaweed, and you will still have a good cooky dough to which you can add some other flavoring.

1 cup flour
Pinch of salt
¼ cup butter
1½ tsp. aonoriko (powdered seaweed)
1 egg yolk
¼ cup sugar
⅛ tsp. baking soda
1 tsp. water

Combine the flour and salt in a mixing bowl. Work the butter in with your hands and blend in the aonoriko. In a separate bowl, beat the egg yolk with the sugar. Dissolve the baking soda in the water and stir into the egg mixture. Work the two mixtures together with your hands. Form the dough into a roll, wrap it in waxed paper, and chill for several hours or overnight. Slice into thin cookies and bake at 350° about 10 minutes or until lightly browned. Makes about 2 dozen small cookies.

Jødekager
(Jewish Cookies)

Jewish cookies are for some reason a Danish specialty. This is my Aunt Helen's recipe, and it was her idea to add the akvavit. I borrow my sister's linie akvavit, the Norwegian kind that travels in freighters across the equator and back and is then marked with the dates of the voyage. But that is an unnecessary refinement. You'll find these cookies unusual and nice to serve with ice cream or puddings.

6 tbsp. butter
⅓ cup sugar
1 egg, separated
½ tsp. grated lemon peel
1 cup flour
⅛ tsp. baking soda
Dash of salt
1 tbsp. akvavit
Cinnamon and sugar
Chopped blanched almonds

Cream the butter and sugar. Beat in the egg yolk and add the lemon peel. Sift in the flour, baking soda, and salt. Add the akvavit. Form the dough into a roll, wrap it in waxed paper, and chill overnight. Slice off thin cookies. Brush each with egg white and sprinkle with mixed cinnamon and sugar and a few chopped almonds. Bake at 350° for 10 minutes or until lightly browned. Makes about 2½ dozen cookies.

Macaroons

Homemade macaroons may sound like a bother, but not the way I do them. The recipe is totally French, but with the American twist of convenience. Rather than pounding the almonds in a mortar, I grind them in the blender, adding only a few at a time to keep the mechanism from clogging. Lining the cooky sheet with foil makes it easy to pry the cookies off afterward. The only problem I cannot eliminate is the sticky fingers you will acquire while molding the macaroons.

    1 cup almonds, blanched
    1½ cups powdered sugar
    1 egg white
    ½ tsp. almond extract
       Pinch of salt
    1 tbsp. apricot jam

Whirl the almonds in the blender a few at a time until finely ground. Transfer to a mixing bowl and stir in the sugar, then the egg white, almond extract, and salt. Put the apricot jam through a sieve and stir into the mixture. Chill the dough for several hours or overnight.

Line a cooky sheet with foil. Form small balls of dough, place them on the foil and press out with your fingers into a flat circle. Flour your hands, for the dough will be wet and sticky. Sprinkle each cooky with a few drops of water and a little additional powdered sugar. Bake at 350° for 12 minutes, or until lightly browned. Slide the foil off the cooky sheet, let the cookies cool and gently pry them off the foil. Makes about 3 dozen small macaroons.

Chinese Almond Cookies

My mother worked out this recipe for almond cookies. They are much better than the ones you get in Chinatown.

2 tbsp. lard
2 tbsp. butter
¼ tsp. salt
⅓ cup light brown sugar
⅓ cup granulated sugar
⅛ tsp. baking soda
1 tbsp. cold water
½ tsp. vanilla
⅔ cup grated almonds (unblanched)
½ cup flour
About 2 dozen whole blanched almonds

Cream the lard and butter. Add the salt, brown sugar, and granulated sugar and beat until light and fluffy. Dissolve the baking soda in the water and add to the creamed mixture with the vanilla. Gradually stir in the grated nuts and flour. Form the dough into balls about the size of a walnut. Place 2 inches apart on a buttered cooky sheet, flatten slightly, and place a whole almond in the center of each cooky. Bake at 350° about 10 minutes, or until lightly browned. Makes from 1½–2 dozen cookies.

7

The Flavor
of Mexico

If you are what you eat, as some people say, then everyone in California is partly Mexican. Out here, Mexican food is as basic as the hamburger. It is eaten in restaurants, at taco stands, or at home, where it may be prepared from scratch, taken out of a can, or thawed from a frozen dinner.

This statewide obsession is to be expected when you consider that California was part of Spain and then Mexico until ceded to the United States by the Treaty of Guadalupe Hidalgo in 1848. Even today, Los Angeles can claim one of the largest communities of Mexican people outside of Mexico City.

If you travel north to San Francisco along El Camino Real (Highway 101), you will pass through such communities as Ventura, Santa Barbara, San Luis Obispo, Paso Robles, Soledad, Gonzales, Salinas, San Jose, Palo Alto, and San Mateo. Now a state like that could hardly be Irish!

In California, we live surrounded by traces of Mexico—Mexican customs, Mexican place names, and people of Mexican origin. The patio, a California institution, came from Mexico and so did the barbecue (barbacoa). On occasion, I have had to speak Spanish in order to make a purchase. And in some restaurants I have heard nothing but the soft ripple of Spanish as it is spoken by Mexicans.

With such a wealth of tradition, it is odd that Mexican restaurants in California seldom explore the heights of their culinary heritage. Occasionally a "mole" or "pipian" will appear on a menu, but ordinarily the basic enchiladas, tacos, and tamales dominate. The most exciting Mexican meals I have eaten in Los Angeles have been those prepared by Mexican-Americans at home.

Nevertheless, everyone has a favorite Mexican restaurant, and arguments over the respective merits of these grow as fiery as the hottest of chiles.

Some of these eating places are excellent. Others are slick franchise operations founded to cash in on our immense appetite for "antojitos" (the typical Mexican snacks) much to the detriment of honest Mexican cookery.

Those who want to prepare the food themselves will find California rich in the ingredients for Mexican dishes. There is scarcely a food item that you can't buy, from epazote, chorizo and queso fresco to the unslaked lime and dried corn required for making tortillas.

Incidentally, the process of making tortillas is the best exercise I have yet experienced. I tried it once using the large rectangular grinding stone that the Mexicans call a metate. First you boil the corn with the lime until the hulls come off, producing "nixtamal." Then you grind the nixtamal on the metate, wearing yourself to a fragment along with the corn. The product of the grinding is a dough called "masa," which you pat into shape and bake on a griddle. I'm a failure at patting out the tortillas by hand, so I do it with a small metal tortilla press that came from Monterrey in the state of Nuevo León.

This process, which I have never repeated, made it clear to me why Mexican women are happy to have their corn ground by neighborhood mills or to buy their tortillas from a "tortillería" or, in a pinch, to make them from the instant masa that requires only the addition of water. Since we have plenty of "tortillerías" in California and most of the supermarkets carry instant masa or packaged tortillas, and since I am not overweight, I have found no reason to grind my own corn again.

Mexican cookery to me is the most exciting in the world— intricate, colorful, and varied. The food is as bright and artistic as the country itself. Indeed, like the pottery, folk art, mosaics, and music, cookery is one more way in which Mexicans express that fascinating personality and flair that I have encountered nowhere else.

If I could eat only one type of food, I would be happy to confine myself to that of Mexico. The following are some of the many dishes that I prepare at home. They are grouped in a way that will make it easy for anyone to become an instant expert in Mexican cuisine. First come bean recipes, then rice recipes, and then the main course. Select one recipe from each category and you will have a typical Mexican meal.

For more elaborate occasions, there are first courses, side dishes, desserts, and beverages and, for the morning after, a typical Mexican breakfast.

TIPS ON MEXICAN COOKERY

Before you start to cook, read carefully the following guidelines. They will help you in dealing with Mexican ingredients.

1. *Chiles.* Use these either fresh or canned, dried or powdered, depending upon what is available. Mexico itself produces close to 100 varieties of chiles, but not all of them are obtainable in any one place. Therefore, each cook adapts the recipes to the chiles grown in her area.

In any case, always test a small portion of chile before using it to see how hot it may be. Then adjust the quantity in the recipe to suit your taste. Neglecting this step can result in a dish so violently hot that it is inedible. I learned this lesson the usual

hard way after throwing out a quart of excellent enchilada sauce—
excellent except that it was of blast-furnace intensity.

If using fresh, long green chiles, always repeat the test, because
sometimes you will find them hotter than others.

Peeling fresh chiles is necessary for most recipes and is easy if
you follow this procedure: Lay the required quantity of chiles in
a pan under the broiler. Then broil until the skins blacken and
blister. When this happens on one side, turn them over and do the
other. Remove the chiles, cut off the stem end, take out the seeds,
and skin them. Then go ahead with your recipe. If you have a
large batch of chiles, you can do them all at once and freeze what
you don't need.

2. *Tortillas.* Both corn and flour tortillas are necessary for these
recipes. The flour tortillas are typical of northern Mexico and the
southwestern United States, but the corn tortillas are basic to
enchiladas, tacos, chilaquiles, and to Mexican cooking in general.

Corn tortillas will crack when rolled for enchiladas unless you
soften them first. This can be done by dipping them in hot
enchilada sauce, which is messy, or by placing them one at a time
in oil heated in a small skillet. It takes very little oil and only a
few seconds to do this. To warm and soften tortillas to eat with a
meal, wrap them in foil and place in a moderate oven for about
15 minutes. Then wrap them in a napkin and serve in a basket
or on a plate.

3. *Beans and Rice.* Basic methods of preparing beans and rice
for Mexican dishes precede each set of recipes. Following them
will guarantee you tasty, tender beans and dry, flaky rice. Use
pinto beans and long-grain raw rice in the recipes.

4. *Lard.* Lard is widely used in Mexico as shortening and as a
cooking agent. Whenever you fry tortillas for a Mexican dish, you
should use lard in order to get the authentic Mexican flavor.

5. *The Garnish.* Even the humblest dish in Mexico is a work
of art in the way it is presented. A flair for design and color seems
to be a national gift. Typical garnishes include strips of avocado,
radishes, olives, grated or crumbled cheese, fried tortilla chips,
shredded lettuce, onion rings and tomato wedges. Fresh flowers
are sometimes used to decorate the plate, and I came across one
cake recipe that called for a rose to be placed in the center. Select
and combine the garnishes according to your own ingenuity.

NOTE: If Mexican ingredients are not available in your area, write to La Victoria Foods, Inc., P.O. Box 309, Rosemead, California 91770. This firm deals in canned chiles, nopales, tomatillos, refried beans, chili powders, Mexican sauces, and other products. They will ship.

BEANS

Basic Bean Preparation

2 cups dried pinto beans
   Hot water
¼ tsp. baking soda
1 large clove garlic
1 medium onion
1 tsp. salt

Cover the beans with hot water and soak overnight. In the morning, drain the beans and rinse. Cover again with hot water and bring to a boil. Add the baking soda just before the boiling point is reached. After the beans reach a full boil, drain them and rinse again.

Now cover the beans generously with hot water. Add the garlic, peeled; the onion, cut in eighths, and the salt. Simmer, covered loosely, for several hours until the beans are tender. Add more hot water as the liquid boils away. When the beans are cooked, proceed with Frijoles Refritos or other recipes.

Dried pinto beans will increase to a little more than twice their bulk when cooked. Two cups dried beans will serve 6–8.

Frijoles Refritos
(Refried Beans)

Some people like their "refritos" soupy, while others cook them until they are dry enough to form into a roll. Whatever your preference, cook them this way.

Follow the method for Basic Bean Preparation, starting with 2 cups dried pinto beans. When the beans are cooked, melt 2 tablespoons lard in a heavy skillet. Lift out some of the beans with a little of their liquid and mash in the lard with the back of a spoon. Continue adding beans and liquid in this manner until all are mashed. Stir in about ½ teaspoon salt and cook until the beans are as dry as desired. Serve very hot and sprinkle about ⅓ cup freshly grated sharp cheese over each serving. Serves 6–8.

Beans with Chorizo

Chorizo gives beans a spicy but subtle seasoning which will make friends wonder how you did it.

Make refried beans according to the above procedure, starting with 2 cups dried pinto beans. Instead of melting lard in the skillet, render out 1 large chorizo and cook until the meat is brown. Add a little extra lard or bacon drippings if the chorizo did not produce enough fat. Now mash the beans and refry with the chorizo and its fat. When the beans are all mashed, add 1 cup grated sharp cheese. Stir until the cheese is thoroughly blended with the beans and cook until the beans are moderately dry. Serves 6–8.

Beans Hacienda

A small restaurant in Nogales, Arizona, turns out good beans that look and taste this way.

Make refried beans, but do not mash the beans thoroughly. Leave some of them whole and stir in enough hot taco sauce to give the beans a distinct touch of "fire."

Spiced Frijoles

Taco seasoning can do wonderful things for other dishes as well. Take these beans, for example.

3 cups cooked pinto beans
½ cup canned tomatoes
3 cups bean liquid (water in which beans were cooked)
1 cup liquid from canned tomatoes
1½ tbsp. taco seasoning mix
1 tsp. salt

Combine the beans with the tomatoes, liquids, and seasonings and simmer, covered, over very low heat for about 6 hours. Check seasoning and add more salt if necessary. These beans will be·quite soupy and should be served in bowls. Makes 4 servings.

RICE

Basic Rice Preparation

Use long-grain rice, allowing 1 cup of raw rice for 4 persons. Place the rice in a saucepan and cover with scalding water. Let stand 15 minutes. At the end of this time, stir and rub the rice a little with your hand. The water will become quite cloudy. Drain the rice and cover with cold water. Stir again and drain. Continue washing the rice in this manner until the water runs almost clear. Then drain the rice and spread it out on a platter to dry.

Begin each recipe by frying the rice in melted lard until the grains are golden. Then proceed with the rest of the recipe, never adding more liquid in the cooking than twice the quantity of raw rice. The liquid should boil up until absorbed by the rice. Then lower the heat and simmer until the rice is dry. At this stage keep the heat very low. An asbestos mat placed under the container will help prevent the rice from burning and sticking.

Arroz Bandera
(Mexican Flag Rice)

The red, white, and green of the Mexican flag blend in the ingredients for this rice.

1 cup long-grain rice
3 fresh long green chiles
1 small onion
½ cup canned tomatoes
1 clove garlic
1 tsp. salt
1 tbsp. lard
¼ cup liquid from canned tomatoes
1½ cups water
Freshly ground black pepper

Soak the rice for 15 minutes in hot water and drain. Wash and drain several times in cold water and spread out to dry on a platter.

Peel and seed the chiles. Cut into strips and chop. Chop the onion and tomatoes. Mince the garlic clove and mash in half of the salt.

Melt the lard in a large skillet. Fry the rice until golden. Add the garlic and onion and cook until the onion is wilted. Stir in the chiles and tomatoes. Add the tomato liquid and water, the rest of the salt, and a sprinkling of pepper. Bring to a boil, then cover, and simmer until the water has been absorbed and the rice is dry and each grain separate. This will take 30–40 minutes. Serves 4.

Arroz Rojo
(Red Rice)

Chili powder, rather than fresh chiles, is used in this rice and helps to give it an appetizing red color. If you are having refried beans, it is nice to save out some of the bean stock for cooking the rice. Otherwise, use water.

1 cup rice
1 tbsp. lard
1 onion
1 clove garlic
1 tsp. salt
½ cup canned tomatoes
1 cup liquid from cooked beans
¾ cup water
½ tsp. chili powder
⅛ tsp. cumin

Soak the rice for 15 minutes in hot water. Drain and wash in cold water until the water runs clear. Drain and spread out to dry on a platter.

Melt the lard in a skillet and fry the rice until golden. Add the onion, chopped, and the garlic, mashed in some of the salt, and cook until the onion is wilted. Add the tomatoes, the liquids, the rest of the salt, the chili powder, and cumin. Cover the rice and bring to a boil. Lower the heat and simmer until the liquid is absorbed and the rice is dry and flaky. Serves 4.

Arroz con Zanahorias
(Rice with Carrots)

Carrots add color to rice that looks innocent but has a touch of fire. Judge the amount of taco sauce by how much heat you can take.

1 cup rice
1 tbsp. lard
1 small onion
1 clove garlic
1 tsp. salt
1 medium carrot
2 tbsp. cilantro
1 tsp. hot taco sauce
  Freshly ground black pepper
  Pinch of cumin
1¾ cups water

Soak the rice for 15 minutes in hot water. Drain and wash in cold water until the water runs clear. Drain and spread out to dry on a platter.

Melt the lard in a skillet or small casserole. Fry the rice until golden. Add the onion, chopped, and the garlic clove, mashed in some of the salt, and cook until the onion is wilted. Grate the carrot, chop the cilantro, and add to the rice. Stir in the hot sauce, the rest of the salt, a sprinkling of pepper, and the cumin. Add the water and boil until the liquid is absorbed. Then simmer until the rice is dry and flaky. Serves 4.

Arroz Rapido

(Quick Rice)

When time is short, you can turn out delicious Mexican rice by this instant method.

1 medium onion
1 clove garlic
½ tsp. salt
1 tbsp. lard
½ cup stewed tomatoes
¾ cup beef stock
½ tsp. chili powder
⅛ tsp. cumin
1 cup instant rice

Chop the onion and mash the garlic in the salt. Cook the onion and garlic in the lard until the onion is wilted. Add the tomatoes, beef stock, chili powder, and cumin. Bring to a boil and add the rice. Cover and set on an asbestos mat or hot plate for 5–10 minutes, or until the rice has absorbed the liquid. Toss with a fork and keep warm until ready to serve. Makes 4 medium servings.

THE MAIN COURSE

Cheese Enchiladas

Enchilada sauces can include anything from soup stock to chocolate and nuts, but there's nothing better than a good basic enchilada featuring lots of rich red tomato-chile sauce, grated sharp cheese, and chopped onions.

THE SAUCE:
  3 cups water
  3 dried California chiles (mild)
½–1 dried New Mexico chile (hot)
  1 tsp. chile.seeds
  2 cloves garlic
  1 cup canned tomatoes
1½ tbsp. lard
  ¼ tsp. cumin
    Pinch of ground cloves
  ½ tsp. salt
  ¼ tsp. freshly ground black pepper

  1 onion
  ⅔ lb. medium Tillamook cheese
  6 corn tortillas
    Oil

To make the sauce, bring the water to a boil. Remove from the stove and drop in the chiles. When the chiles are soft, take them out, reserving the water. Strip the pulp from the outer skin of the chiles. Throw away the stems and all but 1 teaspoon of the seeds. In the blender combine the water in which the chiles were soaked, the chile pulp and seeds, the garlic and tomatoes and blend until smooth. Melt the lard in an earthenware casserole or skillet. Pour in the chile mixture and add the cumin, cloves, salt, and pepper. Simmer for 1 hour, or until the sauce has reduced and thickened slightly. Test for seasoning.

To make the enchiladas, chop the onion and grate the cheese. Soften each tortilla in a little oil heated in a skillet. Place a large spoonful of cheese and onion on one side of the tortilla, roll up tightly and place in a rectangular, shallow casserole or Pyrex dish. Spoon the sauce over the enchiladas to cover thickly. Top with the rest of the onion and cheese. Pour more sauce over and bake at 325° for 25 minutes. Makes 6 servings.

Enchiladas with Brandy Sauce

Enchiladas can reach unexpected heights of elegance as in these baroque creations, the recipe for which came from deep in Mexico. A rich guacamole filling and sophisticated brandy sauce make these ideal for impressive occasions. The tomatillos called for are tiny green tomatoes, which are available in California either fresh or canned.

THE SAUCE:
   2 fresh long green chiles (mild)
   1 dozen tomatillos
   ½ onion
   2 tbsp. chopped parsley
   Salt to taste
   1 tbsp. lard
   2 tbsp. water
   ½ cup half-and-half
   2 tbsp. brandy

THE FILLING:

1 avocado
Juice of ½ lemon
1 clove garlic
½ tsp. salt
2 small tomatoes
1 medium onion
1 tbsp. chopped cilantro

8 corn tortillas
Oil
Grated medium Tillamook cheese
Shredded lettuce, radishes, black olives

To make the sauce, put the chiles, peeled and seeded, the tomatillos, and onion through the food grinder. Add the chopped parsley. Season with salt and cook the mixture in 1 tablespoon lard. When cooked, add 2 tablespoons water, then slowly add half-and-half. Simmer until the sauce is hot. Remove from heat and add the brandy.

To make the filling, peel the avocado and mash with a fork, sprinkling with lemon juice to keep the avocado from turning dark. Mash the garlic clove in the salt and stir into the avocado. Peel and chop the tomatoes; chop the onion and cilantro; and combine these with the avocado.

Soften the tortillas one by one in a little hot oil. Place a generous spoonful of filling on one edge of each tortilla and roll the tortilla tightly around the mixture.

Place the rolled enchiladas in an ovenproof dish. Pour the sauce over. Cover with a layer of grated cheese. Bake in a 350° oven until the cheese has melted and the sauce and filling are hot, about 10–15 minutes. To serve, top with shredded lettuce and garnish with sliced radishes and olives. Makes 8 servings.

Panuchos

Panuchos, a specialty of Yucatán, consist of tortillas split to form a pocket and filled with beans, then fried and topped with meat and sauce. The Yucatán tortillas are small, tender and delicious, and since tortillas have two layers—a thick one and the thin one that puffs up during baking—it is relatively easy to slit and fill them. When you can't get freshly made tortillas, it is easier to skip the slitting and to fry the tortillas whole, spreading the beans on top. The result is actually a type of tostada, but the flavor is just as good. The following recipe is based on panuchos sampled in Mérida and on Cozumel.

Corn tortillas
Lard
Refried beans
Salsa de cilantro (see page 173)
Shredded cooked chicken or turkey

Fry each tortilla in lard until lightly browned. Spread with refried beans. Cover generously with salsa de cilantro and top with shredded meat. Serve immediately. Allow one regular-sized corn tortilla or 2 small ones per person and don't worry about exact proportions in combining the ingredients.

Flautas

Flautas get their name from the flute-like appearance of the rolled, fried tortillas. They are commonly found in southern Arizona, but also appear in California, although sometimes they masquerade here under other names. The combination of chorizo with the shredded beef gives these guacamole-topped flautas a particularly delicious filling.

THE FILLING:
    1 onion
    1 clove garlic
    ½ tsp. salt
    2 tbsp. lard
    2 cups cooked, shredded beef (chuck)
    1 medium chorizo
    2 fresh long green chiles

2 tomatoes
Freshly ground black pepper
¼ tsp. cumin
¼ tsp. oregano

10 corn tortillas
Oil

3 tbsp. lard
Shredded lettuce
Guacamole (see page 172)

To make the filling, chop the onion, mash the garlic in the salt, and cook both in the lard until the onion is wilted. Add the shredded beef to the onion and fry. Remove the casing from the chorizo and fry separately, draining off excess grease. Add the chorizo to the meat mixture along with the chiles, which have been.peeled, seeded, and chopped, and the tomatoes, peeled and chopped. Season with a sprinkling of pepper, the cumin, oregano, and additional salt if necessary. Simmer for 15 minutes.

To make the flautas, soften the tortillas by placing them one at a time in hot oil in a skillet. Place a spoonful of filling at one edge of each tortilla. Roll the tortilla up tightly and tie firmly with string.

Melt 3 tablespoons lard in a large skillet. Fry the flautas in the lard, turning constantly to keep from burning and adding more lard as necessary. Fry until golden. Remove the flautas, pat with paper towels and place in a baking pan. Put them in a 350° oven for about 20 minutes.

To serve, place two flautas on each plate, cover with a handful of shredded lettuce and top with a generous dab of guacamole. Makes 5 servings.

Indios

Mexican cooks produce countless variations on the simple theme of tortillas, cheese, and sauce. All have something in common, but all are different, and they never grow monotonous. Here is one more tasty example.

THE SAUCE:

- 1 tbsp. lard
- 1 clove garlic
- ¼ tsp. salt
- 1 onion
- 2 chorizos
- 4 small tomatoes
- 1 fresh long green chile
  Pinch of cumin
  Pinch of ground cloves
  Freshly ground black pepper
- 3 tbsp. lard
- 8 corn tortillas
- 8 slices Queso Asadero or Monterey Jack cheese

To make the sauce, melt the lard and cook the garlic, mashed in the salt, and the onion, chopped, until the onion is wilted. Remove the casing from the chorizos and fry in another pan until crumbly and brown. Drain off the fat from the chorizos and add the meat to the onion and garlic. Add the tomatoes, peeled and chopped, and the chile, peeled, seeded, and chopped. Season with the cumin, cloves, and a sprinkling of pepper. Taste before adding more salt. Simmer for 10–15 minutes, until the tomatoes are cooked.

Heat 1 tablespoon lard in the skillet to be used for frying the Indios. Dip each tortilla in the lard for a few seconds until soft enough to fold without cracking. Cut slices of cheese the same length as the tortillas. Lay a slice of cheese on one half of the tortilla. Fold the other half over and secure the edges with a toothpick. Add the remaining lard to the pan and fry the folded tortillas until they are lightly browned and the cheese is hot and melting. Cover each tortilla with a generous amount of the sauce to serve. Makes 4 servings.

Sopes

These colorful, multilayered fancies are Mexico's answer to the open-face sandwich. I make my own tortillas in order to get the small size—four to six inches in diameter—which makes them both appetizing and easy to handle.

2 chorizos
2–3 tbsp. lard
8 small tortillas
  Refried beans
  Salsa de cilantro (see page 173)
  Shredded lettuce
  Guacamole (see page 172)
  Queso Enchilado, or other dry, crumbly cheese

Remove the chorizos from their casing. Fry until crumbly and browned. Melt the lard in a skillet and fry each tortilla until lightly browned.

To make the sopes, spread each tortilla with refried beans. Top the beans with a spoonful of chorizo. Next add a layer of salsa de cilantro. Cover with shredded lettuce. Place a dab of guacamole on top of the lettuce and sprinkle with the cheese. Makes 4 servings.

Burritos

Burritos require the big, soft flour tortillas which allow for plenty of filling and can be folded neatly around to make a completely enclosed package. These burritos are made with shredded beef, but you could also fill them with refried beans and cheese. Just remember not to get the filling too wet or the tortilla will disintegrate.

1 clove garlic
1 tsp. salt
1 onion
1 tbsp. lard
2 cups shredded cooked beef (chunk)
1 tomato
1–2 fresh long green chiles
Freshly ground black pepper
Scant ¼ tsp. cumin
Pinch of cloves
4 large flour tortillas

Mince the garlic and mash in ½ teaspoon salt. Chop the onion. Melt the lard in a skillet and fry the onion, garlic and shredded meat until the onion is wilted and the meat is lightly browned. Peel and chop the tomato and the chiles and add. Season with the rest of the salt, a sprinkling of pepper, the cumin and cloves. Simmer for 10–15 minutes.

To make the burritos, place a generous amount of filling just below the center of each tortilla. Fold the bottom of the tortilla over the filling, then fold each side toward the center. Roll the tortilla, folded in this manner, up to the top. Makes 4 burritos.

Quesadillas Avenida Ruiz

As tasty as they are simple to make are these quesadillas that I found in a neat little café on Avenida Ruiz in Ensenada. A clerk in a Tijuana market prescribed the Chester cheese, which has a mild Cheddar flavor and the advantage of softening but not running. Good substitutes are medium Tillamook, mild Cheddar, or Monterey Jack cheese.

3–4 tbsp. lard
8 corn tortillas
8 slices Chester cheese
8 strips green chile
1 onion
Crumbled cheese

Melt the lard in a skillet. Place a tortilla in the lard and on one half of the tortilla set a slice of cheese and a strip of chile. When the tortilla has softened, fold the other half on top of the filling and press down. Continue to fry on both sides until the doubled tortilla is lightly browned. Remove, pat with a paper towel, and keep warm until all the quesadillas are cooked. Serve them topped with rings of onion sliced paper-thin and sprinkled with a crumbly cheese such as the Mexican Queso Enchilado or Queso de Sonora. Makes 4 servings.

Tostada de Monterey

Monterey was the capital of California during the era of Mexican rule, so I wasn't surprised to find there, in a new building flanked by historic adobes, an excellent Mexican restaurant called Zepeda's. This is my version of the beautifully composed tostada that is a house specialty.

    2 tbsp. butter
    1 lb. ground beef
    ½ tsp. salt
    ½ tsp. oregano
    ½ tsp. chili powder
  2–3 tbsp. bottled chili sauce
    1 large avocado
  1–2 tbsp. lemon juice
    2 tbsp. grated onion
    ½ tsp. garlic salt
    1 head lettuce
    3 tomatoes
    2 cups grated medium Tillamook cheese
    4 large corn tortillas
    ¼ cup lard
  1½ cups refried beans

Melt the butter and fry the meat until brown and crumbly, seasoning with the salt, oregano, chili powder, and chili sauce.

Make guacamole by mashing the avocado with the lemon juice and stirring in the grated onion and garlic salt.

Shred the lettuce. Peel the tomatoes and cut in eighths. Grate the cheese.

Fry each tortilla in lard until lightly browned. Build the tostadas by spreading each tortilla with a generous amount of beans and then a layer of meat. Next cover with shredded lettuce. Top this with a generous spoonful of guacamole. Arrange the tomato wedges pinwheel fashion on the lettuce and guacamole and finish with a thick layer of grated cheese. Makes 4 tostadas.

Cazuela de Chilaquiles
(*Chilaquiles in a Casserole*)

Chilaquiles are pieces of tortilla lightly fried and enveloped in sauce. They call them "a poor man's dish" in Mexico, but that is no reflection on the richness of the flavor. Handmade tortillas are better for this recipe because they are thicker and meatier and won't melt away in the sauce.

    8 corn tortillas, preferably handmade
    3 tbsp. lard
    1 medium onion
    1 clove garlic
    1 tsp. salt
    1 (8-oz.) can tomato sauce
    1 cup stewed tomatoes
    ½ cup water
    1 chorizo
    1 tbsp. chili powder
    ½ tsp. oregano
    ¼ tsp. cumin seed
    ¼ tsp. freshly ground black pepper
    ½ cup pitted black olives
    2 cups grated Cheddar cheese
    3 green onions

With kitchen scissors, cut each tortilla into 6 strips and the strips into 3–4 pieces.

In 1 tablespoon lard, cook the onion, chopped, and the garlic, mashed in ½ teaspoon of the salt. Add the tomato sauce, the stewed tomatoes with their liquid, and the water. Remove the chorizo from its casing and fry until crumbly and brown. Add the chorizo to the tomato mixture and season with the chili powder, oregano, cumin, pepper, and remaining salt.

In a skillet, melt 2 tablespoons lard and fry the tortilla pieces until soft and hot, but not crisp.

In a casserole, make a layer of tortilla pieces, a layer of sauce, then some of the olives and cheese. Continue in this fashion until the ingredients are used up. Be sure that the top layer of sauce covers the tortillas well. Sprinkle with more cheese and bake in a 350° oven for 15 minutes, or until the cheese is melted and bubbly and the casserole is heated through.

Garnish with chopped green onions and serve from the casserole. Serves 4.

Carne Asada

Carne Asada is broiled meat, and you may broil it over a wood fire, over charcoal or on the latest of electric appliances. Some Mexican restaurants prepare it this way—topped with strips of fresh chile (canned will do as well). Other necessities are guacamole, refried beans, tortillas, and a bottle of red wine.

    6 steaks
    2 cloves garlic
    2 tsp. salt
      Juice of 1 lemon
    2 tbsp. oil
      Coarse black pepper
    6 fresh long green chiles
      butter

One hour before broiling the steaks, rub them with the garlic, which has been minced and mashed in the salt. Squeeze the lemon juice over the steaks. Add the oil and sprinkle with the pepper.

Broil the steaks to the desired degree of doneness and serve each topped with a mound of chile strips. The chiles should be peeled and seeded, cut in long, thin strips, and warmed in a little butter just before serving. Serves 6.

Chayotes con Carne

Isla de Mujeres is a tiny, palm-trimmed island off the coast of Quintana Roo where you may go for a swim in the bluest of waters and come in, as I did, to a lavish meal featuring chayotes prepared this way.

    2 large chayotes
    1 onion
    2 tbsp. butter
    1 cup stewed tomatoes, drained
    ¼ tsp. oregano
      Pinch of ground cloves
      Pinch of garlic powder
      Salt
      Freshly ground black pepper
    ½ lb. ground beef
    ½ tsp. taco seasoning mix
      Grated Parmesan cheese

Cut the chayotes in half lengthwise. Remove the thin, flat seeds and boil the halves until tender, about ½ hour. Then scoop out the pulp, leaving the shells intact for stuffing.

Chop the onion and cook in 1 tablespoon butter. Add the tomatoes and sprinkle with the oregano, cloves, garlic powder, salt to taste, and pepper. Stir in the chopped chayote pulp.

Brown the ground beef in 1 tablespoon butter and season with a little salt, pepper, and the taco seasoning mix. Combine the beef with the vegetables and heap the shells with this mixture. Sprinkle generously with grated Parmesan cheese and bake at 350° for ½ hour. Serves 4.

How to Make Your Own Tortillas

If you want to make your own tortillas, the most practical method is to use an instant masa such as Masa Harina, which requires only the addition of water. Get the tortillas as flat as possible with whatever means available—hands, a tortilla press, a rolling pin, or a heavy skillet. Place the masa between sheets of waxed paper before pressing. The tortillas won't stick to the paper if you have achieved the proper degree of moisture.

1 cup instant masa
⅓ cup or less water

Add the water gradually to the masa until the dough is moist and spongy—neither dry and crumbly nor soggy. Pinch off a piece of dough about the size of a golf ball. Roll it into a ball, flatten the ball, and place it inside a sheet of waxed paper folded in half. Then press with a tortilla press or other implement.

Peel the tortilla off the waxed paper and place on a very hot un-greased griddle for a minute or two on each side. Don't overcook as this will make the tortillas tough. If the dough begins to dry out, wet your hands and work the water through the dough. This amount of masa will make about 9 tortillas approximately 6–7 inches in diameter.

NOTE: The advantage of making your own tortillas is to vary the size for recipes such as Sopes or Panuchos. It is also possible to work flavorings such as cheese, chili powder and salt through the dough if desired.

THREE SAUCES FOR THE TABLE

Mexicans make their sauces in many ways—some so hot you must be flameproof to consume them. Here are three basic sauces for the table that you can enjoy without an asbestos lining. Guacamole is by now a classic in this country as well as Mexico. Salsa de tomatillos typifies the cooked sauces and salsa de cilantro those which feature chopped fresh ingredients.

Guacamole

True Mexican guacamole does not include mayonnaise or sour cream, which would mask the wonderful freshness of the flavor. Sometimes the avocado will turn dark, other times not—according to its mood, perhaps. But the addition of lemon juice helps to prevent this discoloration which, by the way, does not hurt the flavor at all.

    1 avocado
    1 tbsp. lemon juice
    1 tomato
    2 tbsp. grated onion
¼–½ tsp. chopped hot green chile
    ¼ tsp. garlic salt

Peel the avocado and mash with a fork, pouring over the lemon juice as you mash. Peel and chop the tomato and add together with the onion, the chopped chile, and garlic salt. Mix thoroughly and serve immediately or refrigerate, covered, until serving time.

Salsa de Tomatillos
(*Green Tomato Sauce*)

"Miltomates," "tomatillos," and "tomates de cascara" are various terms for the tiny green tomatoes that, either fresh or canned, are essential for this sauce. When you buy them fresh, they have a parchment-like outer shell (cascara) that the Mexicans boil up in a solution used to improve the texture of tamale dough.

    2 medium tomatoes
    6 tomatillos

2 serrano chiles (small, hot chiles), fresh or canned
⅓ onion
1 clove garlic
¼–½ tsp. salt
1 tbsp. lard

Skin the tomatoes. Wash the tomatillos and remove the outer shell but do not peel. If using fresh chiles, put them in boiling water for a few minutes to soften, then remove the stems, veins, and seeds. Peel the onion and cut in chunks.

Put the tomatoes, tomatillos, chiles, and onion through the food grinder. (Do not purée in a blender, for this sauce is not intended to be a smooth paste.)

Mash the garlic in the salt and stir into the tomato mixture. Melt the lard in a saucepan, add combined ingredients, and simmer the sauce until thoroughly cooked. Test to see if more salt is necessary. Cool and then store in the refrigerator, where it will keep for several days. Serve this sauce as an accompaniment to any Mexican meal. It is also delicious mixed into scrambled eggs.

Salsa de Cilantro

I came across this sauce at Piste, which is just outside Chichén-Itzá in Yucatán. There it was made with the fiery habanero chile and swam in sour orange juice. But I prefer to eliminate these two ingredients and concentrate instead on the simple, perfect relationship of the tomato, onion, and cilantro.

1 bunch of cilantro (about ⅔ cup)
2 medium tomatoes
½ onion
Salt

Wash the cilantro thoroughly. Pick the leaves off the stems and chop coarsely. Peel the tomatoes and chop. Chop the onion. Combine all and sprinkle with salt. Serve on top of Panuchos (see page 161) or as a side dish with Mexican meals.

AN APPETIZER

Tostada de Harina

In southern Arizona and Sonora they make flour tortillas of incredible diameter and so delicate that you can see your hand through them. A southwestern custom is to decorate these gigantic tortillas with cheese, chiles, and anything else available and to serve them as appetizers. The bigger the tortilla, the more dramatic the presentation.

Flour tortillas were popular in early California too, and we can still buy them, either hand or machine made. I like to use either 16 or 20-inch tortillas for this tostada.

> 1 large flour tortilla
> Butter
> Salt
> Grated sharp cheese
> Chili powder

Spread the tortilla with the softened butter. Sprinkle lightly with salt. Make a thick layer of grated cheese over the tortilla. Sprinkle with chili powder—more or less according to how hot you like it. Place under the broiler until the cheese is melted and bubbly. Serve at once, letting each person tear off a portion. Plan on at least 2 of these for 4 people.

THE FIRST COURSE

Ceviche

Non-devotees of ceviche can't seem to accept the idea that soaking raw fish in citrus juice cooks it as surely as if it were poached over heat. One other truism about ceviche is that the more you flavor it the better it will be.

½ lb. lean white fish
Juice of 3–4 lemons
1 tbsp. fresh lime juice
2 tbsp. minced onion
1 medium tomato, peeled and chopped
1 tbsp. minced mild green chile
2 tbsp. chopped cilantro
2 tbsp. oil
5 drops hot pepper sauce
1 tsp. oregano
¼ tsp. basil
⅛ tsp. grated lime peel
½ tsp. salt
¼ tsp. freshly ground black pepper

Shred the fish or cut it into small cubes, place in a bowl, and cover with freshly squeezed, strained lemon juice. Let stand, covered, in the refrigerator overnight. In the morning drain off the lemon juice and rinse the fish thoroughly with cold water. Notice that it is now "cooked." Return the fish to the bowl, stir in the lime juice, and add the remaining ingredients. Chill for several hours.

Serve the ceviche in small bowls or dishes, each lined with a lettuce leaf. Garnish with a wedge of lime. Makes 4 servings.

Fruit Cup Picante

Even the fruit breathes fire in Mexico, at least if it is prepared this way. The sauce that sets the flame should be as hot as you can stand it. As it mingles with the various fruits and their juices, the effect will be safely diminished.

This recipe comes from Margarita Jimenez, who moved to Los Angeles as a bride from her home near San Juan de Los Lagos. Margarita serves the fruit in halves of the tiny cantaloupe that appear briefly in California during the summer.

Choose the fruit in contrasting colors, decorate the arrangement with a mint sprig, and place a hotly colored flower on the side. Then you will have an example of Mexican cuisine at its prettiest.

MIXED FRUIT—4 CUPS:
    Cantaloupe balls
    Watermelon balls
    Pineapple chunks, fresh or canned
    Strawberries
    Grapes, orange segments, peaches, raspberries, etc.

PICANTE SAUCE:
  6 tbsp. pineapple juice
  2 tbsp. fresh lime juice
  ½ tsp. crumbled hot red peppers
    Pinch of salt
  1 tsp. sugar

Soak the sauce ingredients with the hot peppers. If using canned pineapple, the syrup can serve as the juice. Otherwise, use the juice that has drained off the fresh pineapple and sweeten as necessary. Test to see if the sauce is sufficiently burny. Then strain the peppers out and pour the sauce over the mixed fruits. Chill, stirring occasionally. Serve in small cantaloupe halves or in fruit cocktail cups as a first course. Serves 4–6.

THINGS TO DRINK

The best drink to serve with a Mexican meal, in my opinion, is the wine and fruit punch called sangría. I find beer too heavy, and wine doesn't relate well to foods like enchiladas and tacos. Here are three sangrías, depending upon whether you prefer your wine red, white, or rosé. Besides being cool and refreshing, these thirst-quenchers are spectacularly beautiful and provide the sort of color that turns the simplest menu into a fiesta.

Sangría

  1½ quarts red wine
    1 orange
    1 lemon
    1 lime
    ¼ cup orange Curaçao
    3 tbsp. brandy
    2 tbsp. sugar
    2 (7-oz.) bottles club soda
      Ice cubes

Make the sangría about 1 hour before serving. If the wine stands on the citrus fruit too long, it will become bitter.

Slice the orange, lemon, and lime paper thin. Pour the wine over the fruit and add the Curaçao, brandy, and sugar. Stir and taste. The drink should not be too sweet. Cover and chill in the refrigerator. Just before serving, add the club soda and plenty of ice. Makes about 10 servings.

NOTE: Sangría should be brought to the table in a clear pitcher so the fruit can be seen. Include a wooden spoon for muddling the fruit. Serve the sangría in small tumblers or large wine glasses, decorating the edge with a slice of lime or lemon, if desired.

Strawberry Sangría

    1 orange
    1 lemon
    1 cup fresh strawberries
    3 cups rosé wine
    ¾ cup strawberry wine
    ¼ cup brandy
    1 pint club soda
      Ice cubes

Slice the orange and lemon paper-thin and place in a large jar or other glass container with a lid. Add the strawberries, each cut in 3–4 slices depending upon their size. Pour in the rosé, the strawberry wine, and brandy. Cover and chill for 1 hour.

Just before serving, add the soda and ice. Serve over ice in large wine glasses with a few of the sliced strawberries in each glass. Serves 5–6.

Pineapple Sangría

4 thick slices of fresh pineapple
2 limes
1 quart white wine
1 cup pineapple juice
2 jiggers (3 oz.) rum
2 tbsp. orange Curaçao
1 pint club soda
  Ice cubes

Cut the pineapple into chunks, the lime in thin slices. Place in a large jar and add the wine, juice, rum, and Curaçao. Cover and chill.

To serve, pour the sangría into a pitcher and add the soda and ice. Muddle the fruit with a wooden spoon. Serve in large wine glasses or small tumblers, making sure a slice of lime and a few pineapple chunks are in each class. Serves 6.

Café de Olla

The best guide I ever had in Mexico was a Guadalajaran named Elias Mendez. Along with an honest look at life in his country, he gave me this recipe for the sweet, spiced Mexican coffee that gets its name from the earthenware jugs called "ollas."

For each breakfast cup of water, allow 1 level tablespoon ground coffee and ½ teaspoon or more sugar, according to taste. Combine the water, coffee, and sugar along with 1 stick cinnamon in a

coffee pot and cover. Bring to a boil, then pour the coffee off
the grounds, and serve.

DESSERTS

Chongos Barbara

This simply made dessert has such an entrancing flavor that it
is easy to see why it has become a classic in Mexico. I have
eaten "chongos" (curds) in Mexico City and bought them canned
in Tijuana. But when it came to making them at home, I had
such a hard time finding a rennet tablet that I went back over
the border to look for the "pastillas de cuajar" called for in my
Mexican cookbooks. Down in Ensenada, a clerk in a "mercado"
sent me to the corner "farmacia," and there were the pastillas—
made in "Milwaukee."

    1 quart certified raw milk
    2 egg yolks
    ½ rennet tablet
    1 tbsp. water
    1 cup sugar
      Several small pieces cinnamon stick
    2 tbsp. dry sherry

Heat the milk in a large saucepan until lukewarm. Beat the egg
yolks and add. Dissolve the rennet in the water and stir into the
milk. Cover the pan and place on an asbestos mat over very
low heat. The milk should be warmed very gently. Remove from
the burner if it becomes too hot. Let the milk sit until the curd is
thoroughly set and separated from the whey, about 45 minutes to
1 hour. Test by inserting a forefinger into the curd. If the curd
breaks cleanly around the finger, it is ready to be cut.
    Make two intersecting cuts through the curd, dividing it into

quarters. Pour the sugar over the curd and dot with pieces of cinnamon. Place on an asbestos mat over very low heat and let cook without boiling for about 2 hours, or until the curd has thickened and the sugar and whey have formed a syrup. Remove the pieces of curd, or chongos, with a slotted spoon and strain the liquid to remove any fragments of curd. Boil the syrup until reduced by half and add the sherry. Cool, pour over the chongos, and chill. Serves 4–6.

Chocolate Kahlúa Flan

The perfect balance of flavors in this silky flan attests to the Mexican love for sweets. An elegant dessert with overtones of Spain, it can wind up a Mexican meal or formal dinner with equal aplomb and generally provokes a heady amount of compliments.

3 cups milk
½ cup sugar
  Pinch of salt
1 oz. semi-sweet chocolate
2 whole eggs plus 1 yolk
3 tbsp. Kahlúa
½ tsp. instant coffee
½ cup heavy cream, whipped
½ oz. unsweetened chocolate

Bring the milk to a boil with the sugar and salt. Boil, stirring constantly, until the milk is reduced to 2¼ cups. Add the semi-sweet chocolate while the milk is hot and beat with an egg beater to help it dissolve.

When the milk is cool, beat the eggs and add. Stir in the Kahlúa and coffee. Strain the mixture through a sieve. Pour into buttered individual custard cups or molds. Place these in a shallow pan containing 1 inch of water and bake at 325° for 45 minutes, or until a knife inserted in the flan comes out clean. Cool, then chill.

To serve, unmold each flan and top with whipped cream sprinkled with shavings of unsweetened chocolate. Serves 4.

Capirotada

Bread pudding sounds unpromising, but in Mexican hands it becomes a delicacy. The bread pudding called capirotada is traditionally served on Good Friday, but you'll welcome it any time of the year, especially when made this way with brandy, ricotta cheese, and a delicious, cinnamon-spiced syrup.

¼ cup seedless raisins
¼ cup brandy
4 small cones piloncillo
1 cinnamon stick
1 piece lemon peel
¾ cup water
5 slices white bread
¼ cup butter
½ lb. ricotta cheese
¼ cup chopped, toasted almonds

Put the raisins in a saucepan with water to cover and boil until the water is absorbed. Remove from heat, add 2 tablespoons of brandy and let the raisins soak until needed.

To make the syrup, combine the piloncillo, cinnamon stick, lemon peel, and water in a saucepan. Bring to a boil and stir until the sugar cones are dissolved. Continue to boil until the syrup has thickened and is reduced by one-third. Remove from heat. When cool, add the remaining 2 tablespoons brandy.

Lay the bread slices in a baking pan and toast in a 375° oven until lightly browned. Then cut into 1-inch squares. Melt half of the butter in a skillet and toss the bread until it has absorbed the butter. Then add the remaining butter and stir to distribute it evenly among the bread squares.

In a lightly buttered casserole, make a layer of toast squares and then a layer of cheese. Sprinkle with some of the raisins and almonds. Pour a little syrup over. Continue forming layers until the ingredients are used up. Pour in the liquid in which the raisins were soaked.

Cover the casserole and bake at 350° for 45–50 minutes, removing the cover for the last 15 minutes. Serve with cream, if desired. Makes 4–6 servings.

Arroz con Leche y Jerez
(*Rice Pudding with Sherry*)

Rice pudding is a favorite Mexican dessert, and it is delicious whether served plain with a dusting of cinnamon or embellished with raisins, nuts, and wine, as in this recipe.

⅔ cup long-grain rice
2 cups milk
1 cinnamon stick
  Pinch of salt
½ cup sugar
¼ cup seedless raisins
¼ cup sherry
¼ cup chopped, toasted almonds
  Ground cinnamon

Soak the rice in hot water for 15 minutes and drain. Place the rice in a saucepan or top of a double boiler with the milk, cinnamon stick, and salt. Simmer until the milk is nearly absorbed. With a fork, stir in the sugar, raisins and sherry. Continue to simmer until all the liquid is absorbed. Stir in the toasted almonds and serve with a sprinkling of ground cinnamon. Serves 6.

Empanadas de Guayaba
(*Guava Turnovers*)

Empanadas, or little turnovers, are popular from Mexico south to the tip of Argentina. They come stuffed with almost anything—fruit, cheese, beans, or meat. But guava paste gives them that heavenly, pungent, fresh fruit aroma which you never forget once you have visited a Mexican market. The paste, which comes to California markets from Mexico, is sold in slabs, which keep well and are easy to slice.

THE DOUGH:

  2 cups flour
  ¼ cup sugar
  ¼ tsp. salt
  ½ cup lard
  ¼ cup cold water

THE FILLING:

  ¾ cup ricotta cheese
  ¼ tsp. grated lemon peel
 1½ tsp. sugar
  1 tbsp. melted butter
    Guava paste

  1 egg white
    Sugar

Sift the flour with the sugar and salt. Work the lard in thoroughly with the fingers. Add enough of the water to make a workable dough.

To make the filling, mix the ricotta cheese with the lemon peel, sugar, and melted butter.

Form the dough into balls and roll out to a diameter of 5–6 inches. Lay a strip of guava paste on one half of each round. Top with a spoonful of the ricotta mixture. Fold the other edge over, forming a turnover, and seal with egg white.

When all the empanadas are formed, brush each with egg white, sprinkle with sugar, and bake at 350° for about 25 minutes, or until lightly browned. Makes 11–12 empanadas.

Cajeta de Celaya

You might call Celaya, Guanajuato, the candy capital of Mexico. It is famous for cajeta, the soft, brown, caramelly candy that is shipped all over Mexico in traditional round wooden boxes. While goat's milk is a customary ingredient, you can make a perfectly good cajeta without it. I've never tried this recipe without the fig leaf, simply because I have an abundant supply in my back yard.

    1 pint cow milk
    1 pint goat milk
    2 tsp. cornstarch
    ⅛ tsp. baking soda
    1½ cups sugar
    1 cinnamon stick
    1 fig leaf
    1 tbsp. cream sherry

Save out a little milk in which to dissolve the cornstarch. Make a separate solution of milk and the baking soda.

Bring the rest of the milk to a boil. Add the soda and starch solutions, the sugar, cinnamon stick, and fig leaf. Boil, stirring constantly, until the mixture thickens and you can see the bottom of the pan. This will take at least 1 hour. After the first 30 minutes, remove the cinnamon stick and fig leaf.

When the candy is very thick, add the sherry and cook a little longer. Pour into a jar or bowl and cool. The proper consistency of this candy is soft but not fluid. It can be spooned up and eaten plain, spread on crackers, or used as an ice cream topping.

NOTE: If the cajeta should become sugary, turn it back into a saucepan. Add ¼ cup light corn syrup and ¼ cup water. Place over very low heat for about 2 hours, stirring occasionally. When cajeta is smooth, return to storage container.

A TYPICAL MEXICAN BREAKFAST

If the night before included a Mexican dinner, the morning after should find you equipped with leftover refried beans, tortillas, and chile sauce. Heat the beans and decorate them with fried tortilla chips, which you make by cutting tortillas into quarters or eighths and frying them in lard or oil until crisp. Scramble the eggs with the chile sauce. And brew some Café de Olla (see page 178) or Mexican-style hot chocolate. The molletes, or muffins, can be made another time and kept in the freezer for the occasion.

Fresh Papaya, Pineapple or Other Fruit

Frijoles Refritos

Huevos Revueltos con Salsa de Chile

Molletes de Masa

Café de Olla or Hot Mexican Chocolate

Huevos Revueltos con Salsa de Chile
(Scrambled Eggs with Chile Sauce)

Eggs are delicious when flavored with Mexican chile sauce. Add more or less sauce depending upon how hot you can take it first thing in the morning.

  4 eggs
1½ tbsp. cream
  ¼ tsp. salt
  1 tbsp. butter
  2 tbsp. salsa de tomatillos (see page 172) or other chile sauce

Beat the eggs with the cream and salt. Melt the butter in a skillet and add the eggs and stir. As the eggs thicken, stir in the chile sauce and cook until firm. Serves 3–4.

Molletes de Masa

Masa not only serves as tortilla dough but does something special for these Mexican muffins.

3 tbsp. butter
2 tbsp. sugar
1 egg
1 cup all-purpose flour
1 cup instant masa
½ tsp. salt
¼ tsp. cinnamon
1 tbsp. baking powder
1 cup milk

Preheat oven to 400°. Cream the butter and sugar; add the beaten egg. Sift the flour, masa, salt, cinnamon, and baking powder together and add to the butter mixture alternately with the milk. Drop into greased muffin tins and bake at 400° for 20–25 minutes, or until brown. Makes 1 dozen muffins.

Hot Mexican Chocolate

Mexican chocolate should froth like foam on the ocean. There are two ways to achieve this. One is to whip it like the devil with a "molinillo," a stick with a base of revolving parts that one activates by twisting the stick between the palms. An equally effective but less picturesque method of foaming the chocolate is to operate an egg beater with similar vigor.

½ oz. unsweetened chocolate
2 small cones piloncillo
¼ cup water
2 cups milk
1½ tsp. instant coffee
1 stick cinnamon

Place the chocolate, piloncillo, and water in a saucepan over low heat. Stir as the chocolate begins to melt. Add a little of the milk and the instant coffee and beat with an egg beater until all the ingredients are thoroughly blended. Add the rest of the milk and the cinnamon stick and continue beating until the chocolate comes to a boil and is very frothy. Makes 2 servings.

8

A Word on Wine

There's no happier fate for the cook than to live in a state that not only showers one with good ingredients but also supplies their perfect complement—wine.

North, south, and great central valley, California is wine country, with new vineyards and wine producers steadily adding to the riches. As a result, you can pop into a supermarket and buy anything from a premium varietal to an honest jug.

If you don't live here, you can't comprehend the variety. Many wines are not shipped out of the state, and others go in small quantities. Even Californians can't select from the whole gamut, for certain wines are distributed only in the region where they are made and some are sold only at the winery.

That is what makes travel in California fun. You can turn your trip into an impromptu wine tour by stopping in markets and liquor stores to see what strange labels are on the shelves.

You can take a conventional wine tour too. I did it for days, working out of San Francisco. Some of the most beautiful country I visited was the Napa Valley, with its rugged, rolling hills and peaceful vineyards.

Robert Louis Stevenson wrote of Napa and its wine in "The Silverado Squatters." "The smack of Californian earth shall linger on the palate of your grandson," he predicted. Today the vineyard of Jacob Schram, where Stevenson drank Burgundy, Hock, and Golden Chasselas, is called Schramsberg and produces champagne.

To Stevenson, a California vineyard was "one of man's outposts in the wilderness." Things are much more civilized now, and in Napa, wineries line the road as thick as the old Burma Shave signs. Drive along Highway 29 and it's like an open-air premium wine cellar as names like Mondavi, Beaulieu, Inglenook, Heitz, Louis Martini, Beringer, Krug, The Christian Brothers and Hanns Kornell flash by. Stop for a glass of wine at each and you'll never make it through the day.

At some wineries you'll see handsome old buildings. That of Charles Krug is especially picturesque, with its colorful coach house. There is nothing romantic about the warehouse-like structure of Louis M. Martini. But out of that building have come some superb wines, including a treasured bottle of 1957 Private Reserve Cabernet Sauvignon that I have yet to open.

The country around Livermore is flatter and less scenic, but here two great wineries, Concannon and Wente Bros., are practically neighbors across the street. A sign at Concannon informs one that "Grape cuttings from this vineyard were introduced to Mexico between 1889 and 1904 for the improvement of its commercial viticulture." That was a nice thank-you gesture, as grape vines first came to California from Mexico.

In nearby Pleasanton, I lunched at the old, white frame Pleasanton Hotel and was impressed with the wine card, which offered many California bottles. It was a nice change from the toney city restaurants where imported wines are considered chic and California wines something to hide at the bottom of the list. Such snobbism should be boycotted. Far fields are greener only to the ignorant. I like what's going on in my backyard.

Two of the wineries I have seen tie for beauty. One is Korbel, in the spectacular, forested Russian River country. My favorite detective series on television featured an episode photographed in this country, and I'm afraid I was so enraptured with the scenery I forgot to follow the plot.

The other is the Mountain Winery of Paul Masson, which hangs high over the Santa Clara Valley. In the summer you can attend chamber music concerts with the old stone winery as a backdrop. At intermission, you stroll up the tree-studded hill to the champagne bar for a generous sip. Now a state historical monument, the old winery building is used primarily for aging wines. Down the hill in Saratoga, you find the modern Paul Masson Champagne Cellars.

Not far away is Almadén, where Paul Masson got his start. Formal gardens, a zoo containing exotic birds and aging rooms dug out of the earth by Chinese coolies were some of the attractions I saw here.

If I'm especially attached to the Weibel Champagne Vineyards at Mission San Jose, it's because I'm a Stanford University graduate and Leland Stanford built the original winery. You can still see some of the old structure, well bolstered from the inside, of course. A long, tree-lined drive leads to Weibel. And if you continue past, you come to what was once a fashionable resort and later became a residence for alcoholics—an odd neighbor for a winery.

From San Luis Obispo on the coast, the highway turns inland to Paso Robles. In between is rolling ranch country that makes you long for a horse. At Templeton, you turn off to the Pesenti and Rotta wineries. Zinfandel, a grape unique to California, is responsible for the wines here. At Rotta, a small family operation, I've stocked up on jugs of Zinfandel made from a blend reaching back 15 years. My favorite at Pesenti is a premium stock Zinfandel rosé with a refreshing, flowery bouquet.

Heading south to Santa Barbara, you come to the relatively new tasting room of the Santa Barbara Winery. Their Zinfandel, made from Templeton grapes, is an excellent jug red wine. And I feel very Indian when I drink their Sylvaner, a distinctive white wine made from grapes which, the label says, "grow on the slopes of the Sisquoc River."

Southern California also produces a great deal of wine, much of it pretty humble in comparison to the sleek Chardonnays, Pinot

Noirs and Cabernet Sauvignons of the north. But wine touring in this area is fun too.

Between Cucamonga and Etiwanda I found a curiosity of a wine called Cesare's Bordolese. "It is smooth like silk," enthused the proprietor. "It will bubble in your glass like champagne." Now who could resist a sales pitch like that?

Located just off the freeway is the vineyard of Joseph Filippi. Driving through vines hanging with Grenache grapes, I came to a small tasting room where I was taught how to approximate an expensive cherry liqueur. You take a Filippi specialty called Marsovo, which is a Marsala-type dessert wine, and mix it half and half with cherry wine. The result is delicious.

Practically next door at Guasti is the Brookside Vineyard Company, an enterprise with not only vineyards but tasting rooms scattered over southern California and more tasting rooms in the north. Brookside produces a large variety of wines, including the Assumption Abbey label that is bottled under the auspices of Benedictine monks.

I have to thank Brookside for stocking the only glasses I have been able to find that are appropriate to sherry. Sherry should not be served in the inverted triangle-shaped glasses usually offered. A small version of the tulip glass with a short stem is more like what they use in Spain.

There's wine making in Los Angeles too. One of my favorite places in the city is the San Antonio Winery. I learned about it years ago on the chairlift at Mammoth Mountain. (Skiers are great wine fans.) At San Antonio, you receive a personal welcome from the Riboli family, and you can follow a line on the floor for a self-conducted tour. If you come at harvest time, you can watch the crushing.

San Antonio was the last producing winery in Los Angeles until the Navé Pierson Winery opened up. Both are in the downtown industrial district, where the scenery is best forgotten. But you don't need scenery when there is good wine to drink.

I first tasted wine at the age of ten, when I found a bottle of port on a night stand, tipped it up, and then tipped it up again. Now with a start like that, who could be snooty about wine? The best advice I have for would-be connoisseurs is to take wine off its pedestal and enjoy it. Don't be ashamed if you lack knowledge. You can only learn about wine by drinking it, which means the more you have to learn the better!

There are certain techniques, however, that will help you to develop a discriminating palate. One is to taste two wines of the same type, for example two Pinot Chardonnays from different makers or two Pinot Noirs, together. When you taste one wine alone, you have no standard against which to judge it. When you taste two, the contrast helps highlight the features of each.

Try comparing only the bouquets before you actually taste the wines. If you concentrate, you will find that you can quickly identify each wine by its bouquet and that if someone mixed up the glasses, you could easily sort them out. This will prove to you that tasting wines is not a matter of hocus-pocus. The differences are as definite as black and white. All it takes is experience.

There is no need to reach the level where you can taste wines blindfolded and identify them by type, vineyard, and vintage year. That is showmanship, not enjoyment. I only managed it once, when I correctly identified Gallo Vin Rosé in a blind tasting. There would have been something wrong with me if I hadn't. During my early skiing career, this rosé was practically the only wine my friends buried on the slopes. I drank rivers of it.

Don't be overly analytical when you taste wine. Just figure whether you like it or not and then tell yourself why. Forget the fancy wine vocabularies and use your own words. Also, keep a wine notebook. Write down the wines you buy, your opinion of them, the foods you serve them with, and whether you like the combination. Don't think you need to be a walking dictionary of wine lore or that you must be able to evaluate the finest nuance of every wine technically and knowingly. Only men in the wine business need such expertise. It's crucial to the decisions that earn them a living. They also have more opportunities to taste.

When you pour a wine, study its color first, and then the bouquet. Swirl the wine around, put your nose way into the glass, and take a good sniff. Experts next take a little in the mouth and swish it about, slurping in some air at the same time. I won't attempt to describe this process because the first time I saw it, I practically collapsed on the floor, trying to keep my own face straight. If you want some idea of what it looks like, study the mirror the next time you rinse your mouth after brushing your teeth.

When it's an occasion for serious tasting, not socializing, the experts don't swallow the wine, they spit it out. I learned the wisdom of this on a wine tour of California, when in one day I tasted some seventeen wines plus champagne and cocktails. But I didn't have the nerve to try it until I was in Bordeaux. Here I watched Jean Cruse, one of the local champions in the art, pitch a bit of Chateau d'Yquem neatly over the tail of the cellar master's dog. Later that day I was in the dank cellars of Chateau d'Issan. Twilight fell, no one was around, and I slunk behind a barrel and had my turn.

Collecting wine accessories can be an absorbing and expensive hobby, but all you really need is the right glassware. The wrong glasses can actually ruin the effect of a wine. I had a dramatic demonstration of this from a French champagne maker. He poured out two helpings of his wine, one in the flat, saucer-like glass we think of as traditional for champagne and the other in a tall, narrow tulip glass. If I hadn't known, I would have thought I was looking at and tasting two different wines. The champagne in the saucer glass was pale, lifeless and lacked bouquet. That in the tulip glass showed good color, a steadily mounting column of firm bubbles, and a deep, wonderful bouquet. The broad, flat glass dissipated all the attributes of the wine. The narrow glass concentrated them.

You can collect glassware of all sorts—expensive imported crystal, huge Burgundy balloons, glasses with smaller, rounded bowls for white wines, and so forth. Actually, you need only one type of glass, the so-called all-purpose glass with a generous bowl that curves in slightly at the top to hold in the bouquet. Whatever you have, it should be clear and colorless. The idea is to admire the color of the wine you are drinking, not the tint of the glass. And you should never fill the glass. Let the wine come only part way up, leaving plenty of room for the bouquet to circulate.

Naturally, when the right glassware is not available, you accept the paper cup, water tumbler or whatever and enjoy its contents. Wine is meant to be lived with, not worshipped. Some wineries offer only paper cups or plastic glasses in their tasting rooms. That's bad, because you can't seriously taste from paper or plastic. But then, life holds deeper problems, like who's going to do the dishes?

Now, about the rules for wine drinking. Let them serve as guidelines, not obstacles. That business about red wines with red meat and white wines with fish or fowl is helpful, but it's not the whole truth. A sweet white wine would be horrid with roast beef, of course. But there are times when you can serve a red wine with chicken, for example, if it is prepared with a hearty red wine sauce. A delicate cream sauce would take a white wine. I lunched with winemakers in Spain and saw them choose red wine with fish. The reason? They considered the Spanish red wines superior to the whites and the quality of the wine they were drinking more important than the character of the dish.

Many people, men as well as women, do not care for dry red wines. The solution here is obvious. If a wine disagrees with you or displeases you, don't drink it. I talked about this with a stevedore who was also a wine fancier. His favorite dinner was steak and lobster. Now you can't win with a combination like that. Half of it takes red wine and half white. But this rugged man never hesitated. He ignored the dilemma and followed his own convictions. His choice: an Emerald Riesling, a fruity white wine that he preferred with most foods.

Wine really doesn't go with some meals. It is terrible, for example, with Mexican food. I tried a robust Zinfandel with a Mexican dinner, and the strong flavors of the food and the wine cancelled each other out. But the French wouldn't give up in a situation like that. They'll match their wines with anything.

A delegation from Bordeaux, visiting California, was treated to an authentic Mexican meal—not the typical restaurant variety of food but some sophisticated, complex dishes. "Trop epicié" ("too spicy"), they complained as they picked at the food. But they thought Americans might try such wild concoctions with a sweet wine, possibly a Sauterne.

Strong foods, such as curries, Mexican dinners, Southeast Asian foods, and the spicier Chinese dishes, tend to blot out the flavor of wine. But they weren't designed to go with wines anyway. Dining in a Chinese home, I saw an interesting compromise. The hostess served a medium dry California flor sherry. Her choice made sense, as shao shing, the Chinese rice wine, has a faintly sherry-like taste.

Wines should be served at the proper temperatures. White wines and rosés are more appetizing if chilled, and reds have their full flavor at room temperature. However, there are times when I cannot drink a red wine comfortably. If the night is hot and stuffy, it chokes me like cotton in the mouth.

White wines should not be chilled to the point of numbness. Some say two hours in the refrigerator is sufficient. And a wine authority I know prefers them just below room temperature, the better to savor their qualities. I like white wines cold enough to frost the glass. That chilly look over green-gold glints is infinitely appealing. But I admit I get more flavor with the last swallows, when the wine has warmed up.

If company comes and someone brings a white wine for the dinner, there is always an emergency solution to chilling it—five minutes in the freezer.

And now, a word for water. I have been to gourmet society dinners where ash trays were swept from the tables and even mention of water was taboo. But my physiology is only human, not epicurean, and sometimes the rich foods and alcohol add up to such a thirst that I cannot continue without a taste of this maligned liquid. Only wine snobs would be rigid enough to deny such a thirst.

Now let's take the opposite position. Say water, beer, or Hawaiian punch has been your primary mealtime beverage. How do you get acquainted with wine? That's simple. You go to the liquor store and buy a bottle. But which bottle? That depends upon what you are having for dinner. Don't worry about the vast array of imported bottles with strange sounding labels. I am limiting this discussion to California wines, as they are excellent and will give you the best bargain for your money. There is no need to tackle the Bordeaux and Burgundies right off the bat, particularly if your French is a little rusty. I've seen more people mumble over wine lists or avoid them entirely because they couldn't pronounce the names.

But back to dinner. You are going to have steak, hamburgers, spaghetti, lasagne, pot roast, beef bourguignon, leg of lamb, or roast beef. All of these take a red wine. But you look at the bottles and see, among the reds, Cabernet Sauvignon, Pinot Noir, Gamay, Gamay Beaujolais, Burgundy, Zinfandel, Charbono, Petite Syrah, Barbera, Chianti and a few more. How do you select the right one for your meal? First, you put the idea of only one right wine out of your head. Then you read the labels. Many indicate the types of food which go with the wine. You can also ask the sales clerk. He should have some fundamental information, and in a good store, may be quite knowledgeable. If you enjoy the wine and think it pairs well with your meal, you repeat it. If not, you try another wine the next time. Choosing a wine is not the life-and-death matter the high priests of wine snobbism would have you think it is. Perhaps a Cabernet Sauvignon is too grand a wine for spaghetti, but combining them is not a catastrophe.

Another matter: don't worry about a vintage date on the label of a California wine. The vintage date is nothing more than the year the grapes were harvested. It can appear on the label only if all the grapes used in the wine were harvested and crushed that particular year. Wines without a date are a blend of years, but they are not necessarily superior or inferior to the dated wine. You don't need a vintage chart for California wines. There are climate variations from year to year, but they are not as crucial to the quality of the wine as in Europe.

Now we'll move on to white wines. Here again you have a multitude of choices—Pinot Chardonnay, Pinot Blanc, Chablis, Sylvaner, Traminer, Gewurztraminer, Chenin Blanc, Rhine, Johannisberg Riesling, Semillon, Sauvignon Blanc, Green Hungarian and so on. Some are dry and crisp; others are fruity; and some have a touch of sweetness or spiciness. Here again, you must learn by trying.

I'll admit it can be confusing because wines of the same variety can be quite different. For example, a Chenin Blanc can be sweet or dry. If made by Louis M. Martini or Mayacamas Vineyards, it will be dry. But if it comes from Weibel, The Christian Brothers, Mirassou Vineyards or Charles Krug, it will be slightly sweet. Again, check the labels and look for such words as dry, semi-dry, or mellow. Mellow usually indicates a softer wine, often on the sweet side.

Sometimes you just have to take a chance. The greatest wine

dilemma I've experienced involved an Australian Sauterne which was titled Chardonnay. In California, Chardonnay is the Pinot Chardonnay, which produces a dry white wine. In France, a Sauterne is a sweet wine. And a California Sauterne can be either sweet or dry. (Generally the word "haut" is attached to a Sauterne if it is sweet.) I served this puzzling wine with a Chinese dinner. It turned out to be slightly sweet, but far from a dessert wine, and worked out well with that particular menu.

Rosés are often served as a compromise. A rosé will go with anything, you are told, and is safe if you are in doubt about what to serve. Those who do not like dry red wines will offer a rosé as an alternative with a steak or chops. Or if a group dines out and one person orders steak, another chicken, a third sole, and a fourth lamb, a rosé is supposed to be the tactful choice.

Judging by the way it is used, rosé stacks up as an insipid, meaningless wine. That is slighting treatment for a wine that can be delightful under the right circumstances. Rosés are light wines, and many of them tend to be sweet. They should be served as luncheon or warm weather wines with the same type of foods you would accompany with a slightly sweet white wine.

I have found some rosés that, to my tastebuds, had character. Buena Vista's Rose Brook Cabernet Rosé is one and Assumption Abbey's Vin Rosé another. I also like the Grignolino Rosé from Heitz Cellars and the Mountain Rosé by J. Pedroncelli. Among the sweeter rosés, I favor the premium stock Zinfandel Rosé made by Pesenti. (Unfortunately, it is not distributed very widely. I can't get it even in Los Angeles.) I also like Paul Masson's Pink, Almadén's Mountain Nectar Vin Rosé, and Mirassou Vineyards' Petite Rosé.

In naming specific wines, I don't mean to set myself up as a judge. I just mention what I've enjoyed, not what I think are the finest California wines or even the finest from a particular winery. I can't speak for the whole range of California wines, because I haven't tasted them all. That means I have many exciting dis-coveries to make, and when I go into a wine store, I browse among the labels as others would browse through books.

California white wines offer tremendous possibilities for en-joyment. Some that I like are the Pinot Blancs from Wente Bros.,

Mirassou Vineyards, and the Novitiate of Los Gatos. I like Weibel's Chablis, Pinot Chardonnay and Chenin Blanc. And the first great Chenin Blanc I tasted was from Mayacamas Vineyards. Wente Bros.' Grey Riesling is a big seller and a pleasing, slightly spicy wine. From Wente's neighbor, Concannon, I choose the Moselle and Johannisberg Riesling. A Johannisberg Riesling made by Souverain Cellars is a rare find, and one from Llords & Elwood is exceptional. Almadén's Gewurztraminer is nice for a sweet wine. And lots of men I know go for Paul Masson's Emerald Dry. Among champagnes, Almadén's Blanc de Blancs is tops with me.

Red wines I find pleasing include the Beaumont Pinot Noir from Beaulieu Vineyard, the Ruby Cabernet and Cabernet Sauvignon from Heitz Cellars, Weibel's Pinot Noir, Royal Host's Select Premium Burgundy and the Mountain Zinfandel from Louis M. Martini. I was lucky enough once to taste a well-aged Cabernet Sauvignon from Inglenook. It was a beautiful experience. Beyond these, you can take your pick from a long string of Pinot Noirs and Cabernet Sauvignons. What I have named is only a drop in the wine bucket.

Most California wines are moderately priced. Some are expensive. But there are also many good buys in low-priced wines. Louis M. Martini offers good value in inexpensive Mountain Red and Mountain White wines. Brookside's Hausmarke Rhine is a delightful flowery white wine. And a few years back I bought a fifth of CK Mondavi Rhine Wine for only eighty-nine cents and branded it as one of my favorites.

Also on my low-priced list are Samuele Sebastiani's Mountain Red and Concannon's Livermore Red. Korbel is putting out a line of moderately priced wines in half-gallon bottles. Almadén does an excellent job with its Mountain Rhine Wine and Mountain Nectar Vin Rosé. And Le Domaine, which is made by Almadén, is a terrific buy in champagne.

False ideas can ruin much of the fun of wine drinking. I had an excellent Johannisberg Riesling at a luncheon once and was surprised when the hostess apologized for the wine. It wasn't dry enough, she said, as if dryness alone were a virtue. Some wine experts acknowledge the sweeter wines as good for novices who, as they gain experience, will surely progress to drier wines. Well, what if you don't want to progress? You have my sympathy, as I'm all for the individualist. There are also plenty of dinner wines that will please you.

Among the sweeter white wines are Wente Bros.' Le Blanc de Blancs, Paul Masson's Rhine Castle, Almadén's Gewurztraminer and Mountain Rhine Wine, Llords & Elwood's Johannisberg Riesling, Weibel's Green Hungarian, The Christian Brothers' Sauvignon Blanc and the Chenin Blancs from Charles Krug, The Christian Brothers, Mirassou Vineyards, and Weibel.

I have already suggested some sweeter rosés. And most of the rosés you find will be soft enough to please you anyway.

Red wines are more difficult. There are sweet Zinfandels from wineries like Rotta and Pesenti, but you won't find those outside of California or many places in California. Guild's Vino da Tavola is on the sweet side and also Brookside's Hausmarke Rote. Another idea is to go to Italian markets and look for red wines labeled mellow or vino rosso.

Certain red wines are not sweet but seem easier on those who don't like dryness. These include Paul Masson's Rubion and Baroque and the cabernet sauvignons from Llords & Elwood and Heitz Cellars.

Then there is the whole range of dessert wines including angelica, the sweet Sauternes, ports and sherries, muscatel, tokay, and the so-called "chateau" wines such as Chateau Wente, Chauteau Concannon, and so forth.

Some of the muscat-flavored wines are delightful. I remember especially a delicate moscato amabile from Bargetto. I found it in a tasting room on Cannery Row in the midst of the abandoned sardine canneries immortalized by John Steinbeck. Louis M. Martini is also known for a wine of this type.

There are many fruit wines too, including such unusual varieties as olallieberry wine. My favorite among the fruit wines is apricot wine. And the best apricot I have found is that made by the Santa Barbara Winery under its Solvang label (Solvang is the nearby Danish community). You think you are eating the beautifully perfumed fresh fruit when you drink it. Other good apricot wines come from Bargetto and San Martin.

I'm not going to mention the wildly flavored sweet novelty

wines that have been put on the market. I'm sure they have their place, but it isn't in my cellar.

You can get bad wines in California. And by bad I don't mean inferior bottles, but wines with peculiar, off flavors. This happens primarily when you buy from out-of-the-way vineyards. I have purchased some raw bottles of Claret (at sixty-nine cents a half gallon) and perfumy Burgundies. Possibly the worst was a Yugo-slavian-type wine I found in San Pedro, the home port for many Yugoslavian fishermen. While there was no hope for this wine at the table, I managed to turn it into an excellent sangría. The fruit, sugar, and other flavorings used in this wine punch drowned out the defects. But if you have a wine that has turned to vinegar from oxidation and poor storage, there can be no happy ending. The best place for it is the kitchen drain.

Part of the fascination of wine is its variability. What seemed fantastic to you one time may seem ordinary the next. The wine isn't at fault here. It is the circumstances under which you drink it. Wine is a creature of mood and atmosphere, food and friends, all of which color your reaction to it.

Don't let California wines be spoiled for you by conditioning of another sort. Here I refer to the wine prigs who would have you believe that a good California wine can never equal a good European wine. I've read books by people like this. They'll praise wines from the farthest reaches of the world before they'll mention California. Then their words are either condescending or critical. If you believe what you read, you can easily develop an inferiority complex about domestic wines—like the hostess who was praised for the quality of the California wines in her pantry and gasped, "But I only use those for cooking!"

An elegant wine store in a wealthy neighborhood of Los Angeles features a wide selection of California bottles as well as high-priced European wines. But snob appeal is so powerful that many of the best bottles are left on the shelves, said the proprietor, referring to the California wines.

Unfortunately, some of our winemakers seem to imply that something is lacking with our product. I refer to those who christen their wines with names like "fumé blanc" or "blanc de blancs." These are French terms, and using them implies we have an inferiority complex about our wines and must latch onto French prestige to make them sell.

The French aren't crazy about some of our terminology either. For example, they insist we do not make champagne. The only true champagne, they say, is that made in the Champagne district of France.

We've used generic terms like Claret and Burgundy in California for ages. These terms don't bother me. Although they may strictly apply only to French wines, they have become part of our language in the same way as words like matinee and chic. Actually, neither of these terms is French to begin with. Claret is the name the English gave to the wines of Bordeaux. And although we speak of Burgundy as one of the great wine regions of France, there is really no such place. In France it is La Bourgogne.

The idea of rivalry between French and California wines is silly. We praise the great wines of France, Germany, and other countries and our own too. There is really no basis for comparison, as each country has different soil, different sun, and a different product. We are grateful to Europeans for the help they have given us. Our first grape vines came from Mexico with the Spaniards who settled California. And the winemakers who made our vineyards flourish came here from France, Germany, Italy, and other countries. French winemakers study at the University of California at Davis, a great center for research in enology. And Californians go to France to learn.

When the dread blight phylloxera attacked the vineyards of Europe in the last century, American root stock came to the rescue. And vine cuttings from France grow in California vineyards. I saw cuttings from Chateau d'Yquem in the Livermore vineyards of Wente Bros. And a cutting from Chateau Margaux thrives in my own garden.

It's embarrassing how that came about. After a visit at the chateau, I was handed a clump of a fern-like plant in a paper bag. Never one to throw away scraps of paper, string, or anything else with a sentimental attachment, I crammed it in my suitcase for two more weeks of hectic travel. When customs in New York asked if I had any plant material, I said a perfectly honest no, as I had completely forgotten the incident. It was a shock to find the shriveled, dried little clump when I unpacked. It was a greater shock when green sprouts appeared after I soaked it in water.

In 1967, Los Angeles was named a sister city of Bordeaux. In the same year I was named a "gourmette du vin de Bordeaux" in a ceremony in France. Dressed in heavy velvet robes, I nervously went through the rites conducted by the Grand Conseil du Vin de Bordeaux. The crucial test was to identify a glass of wine. I looked at the wine, sniffed it, tasted it carefully, and gave my response. "It's a red wine," I said. And the gentlemen applauded.

So you see, wine can inspire good humor and good fellowship around the world. In my cellar—that's a fancy word for closet— there are scores of California bottles, but also great wines from Bordeaux and Burgundy, Alsatian wines, sherries from Spain, a selection of Mexican wines that I brought up through Nogales, Portuguese wines, Australian wines, and a bottle from South Africa.

I believe one should take advantage of all the good the world offers. And no matter who makes it, wine is a fascinating beverage and a delightful adjunct of good living. It's funny so much egotism, prejudice, and snobbery have grown up around it. For wine itself is a friendly drink, ready to confer its benefits upon anyone who will approach it with enthusiasm and an open mind.

9

Menus from a
California Kitchen

Dining California style means to me a succession of imaginative, savory menus that make the most of the different culinary styles and exciting foods available to our kitchens.

Friends of mine are shocked to find that I serve what they consider company meals (by definition, anything which takes a little thought) for my own pleasure, and not just when they are invited. But if I refused to honor my own stomach, how could I possibly be fit to honor theirs?

It is a shame that so many believe preparing a carefully seasoned meal from scratch requires an impossible outlay of time and money and is something to be done only on rare and very special occasions.

The idea that more or less palatable slop should be served for everyday indicates to me something other than thrift, for one can eat simply but magnificently and treat the most humble foods with a respect that makes them suitable for a feast. More plausible reasons for slighting food are laziness, lack of ingenuity, and that old idea that it is wicked to make the basic aspects of life pleasurable. Sadly enough, the stomach, once convinced that its most enjoyable activities are sinful or, at best, frivolous, will react with a painful guilt complex of its own.

If I am particular about food, I am also particular about my guests. It takes talented and receptive diners to inspire a cook. Who wants to express oneself in a beautiful meal only to watch a sickly fussbudget weed out some offensive ingredient?

Wine is an essential part of my dinners. I always select the bottle to harmonize with the food and often to tie in geographically with a particular menu—a Rioja wine with a Spanish meal, a Mexican wine with certain Mexican foods and an Australian wine with dishes from across the Pacific. I believe in sampling as many of the world's good things as possible, especially when they are available so close to my doorstep.

The bulk of the wines I serve, however, are from California. They offer range and quality enough to please anyone but a wine snob. The meal I present with an imported wine one time will appear with a California wine the next. I also like to pair wines from at home and abroad on the same menu.

Another of my pleasures is to dress the table with accessories that set off the food. I have gathered placemats from all over the world—Jamaica, Manila, Bangkok, Japan, Finland, Portugal, Mexico, and Guatemala. Two lengths of batik brought from Indonesia by a friend required only a seam up the middle to become a handsome and unusual tablecloth.

My dishes are also international. Silver-rimmed white china from Japan makes a good background for any meal. Company Mexican dinners are served on handpainted pottery from Tlaquepaque, each piece featuring a different design. Rough, yellowed plates from Tzintzuntzan, decorated with animal motifs and signed by the artist, lend atmosphere to everyday Mexican meals. If the menu is Oriental, I have blue-and-white, rice-patterned bowls from Hong Kong and mistily painted Japanese plates which I found, of all places, over the border in Tijuana.

The colors I select for the table depend upon which flowers are in bloom. I like especially to feature displays of brilliant, ruffly hibiscus—pink, golden orange, or deep red according to which bush is doing the best. When no flowers satisfy my mood, I'll center the table with a brass spray of pomegranates from Hong Kong, a black bowl from Patzcuaro heaped with clay fruit from Guatemala, or a Pueblo Indian bowl holding dried weeds from the California desert.

All this is only personal whim, for a meal can be equally appetizing, or more so, on an oilcloth-covered table flanked by hungry, cherished, and cheerful friends.

Now, on to the menus. All of the recipes are included in the book except for such standards as baked ham and roast lamb, and the wines not from California are marked with their place of origin. The menus are not necessarily intended for exact duplication but to illustrate a philosophy of dining and to show how a willingness to try something different can make the dinner hour the most interesting of the day.

A CALIFORNIA MEXICAN MEAL

Ensalada de Cacahuates

Steaks with Wine and Chile
Chayotes Stuffed with Spinach
Arroz con Zanahorias

Chongos Barbara

THE WINE
Paul Masson Rubion

DINNER IN THE SOUTHWEST

Margaritas and Tostada de Harina

Cazuela

Flautas
Arroz Rojo
Beans Hacienda

Capirotada

THE WINE
Strawberry Sangría

A RANCHERO DINNER

Carne Asada
Frijoles Refritos
Arroz Bandera

Chocolate Kahlúa Flan

THE WINE
Casa Madero San Carlos 1964 (a red wine from
Parras de la Fuente, Coahuila, Mexico)

AN ORIENTAL PARTY

Saketinis and Shortcut Rumaki

Tofu Vegetable Tapestry

Ginger Spareribs
Chinese Vegetable Bake
Steamed White Rice

Gula Malacca

THE WINE
Concannon Moselle

A MENU FROM THE PACIFIC

Cucumber Sunomono

Five Fragrance Chicken
Toss Fried Cauliflower, Chinese Style
White Rice

Almond Curd with Fresh Coconut
Chinese Tea

THE WINE
Seppelts Chardonnay Sauterne (Victoria, Australia)

FOODS FROM THE FAR EAST

East First Street Suimono

Ginger Beef Frank Wong
Chinese Vegetable Bake
Fried Rice

Minted Longans
Chinese Tea

THE WINE
Brookside Hausmarke Rhine

DINNER IN SPAIN

Dry Sherry with Salted Almonds and Green Olives

Consommé al Jerez

Cordero Asado (Roast Lamb)
Herb Baked Carrots
Chip Potatoes

Spanish Orange Cream

THE WINES
The aperitif:
Tío Pepe Fino Sherry (Jerez, Spain)
Added to the soup:
Williams and Humbert Dry Sack Sherry (Jerez, Spain)
Served with the lamb:
Cune Rioja Clarete Cosecha 1962 (Compañía Vinicola
del Norte de España, Haro-Bilbao, Spain)

Used in the dessert:
Christian Brothers Golden Sherry
Served with the dessert:
Chateau Concannon

DINNER IN LOS ANGELES

Guacamole Soup

Steaks with Sherry-Oyster Sauce
Sesame Carrots
Baked Potatoes

Mango Rum Charlotte

THE WINE
Heitz Cellars Cabernet Sauvignon

SUNDAY DINNER

Crunchy Pear Salad

Chicken Sebastopol
Chayotes with Bacon
Garlic Mashed Potatoes

French Rum Cream

THE WINE
Wente Bros. Le Blanc de Blancs

A MENU FOR EASTER

Sweet-Sour Wine Mold

Baked Ham
Lima Beans with Dill
Potatoes and Onions

Coeur à la Crème with Strawberry Port Sauce

THE WINE
Weibel Extra Dry Champagne

DINNER, DANISH STYLE

Carrot-Brandy Soup

Danish Steak with Onions
Boiled Potatoes with Butter and Parsley
Seasoned Spinach

Aunt Helen's Danish Buttermilk Soup

THE WINE
Chateau Pontet Canet 1962 (Bordeaux, France)

FLAVORS OF SOUTHEAST ASIA

Curry Soup

Beef and Water Chestnuts
Indonesian Coconut Rice
Chilled, Sliced Cucumbers

Vermicelli Sorn Daeng

THE WINE
Buena Vista 'Rose Brook' Cabernet Rosé

AN ORIENTAL SUPPER

Longan Cucumber Relish

Japanese Chicken in Foil
Sherried Rutabaga
Boiled Rice

Jasmine Tea with Chinese Almond Cookies and
Chinatown Coconut Candy

THE WINE
Wente Bros. Pinot Blanc

A COLLECTION OF MENUS BUILT AROUND A ONE-DISH MAIN COURSE

Chicken-Chile Soup, Mérida Style
Chayotes con Carne
Peach Clafoutis

THE WINE
J. Pedroncelli Mountain Rosé

Mexican Flag Salad
Black Bean and Chorizo Soup
Dulce de Coco

THE WINE
Assumption Abbey Vin Rosé

Caesar Salad Boccaccio
Wine Country Linguini
Peaches with Orange Sherry Cream

THE WINE
Louis M. Martini Mountain Zinfandel

Ceviche
Cazuela de Chilaquiles
Orange Shells with Native Cheese

THE WINE
Sangría

Potage Parmentier
Pork Chops with Prunes and Wine
Albert's Swiss Apple Pie

THE WINE
Almadén Gewurztraminer

Greens with Lemon Dressing
Pozole Casserole
Almond-Peach Atole

THE WINE
Samuele Sebastiani Barbera

Anchovy Pepper Salad
Mexican Shells
Cuban Bananas in Wine

THE WINE
Heitz Cellars Grignolino Rosé

Index